SURVIVAL PLUS

By the author:

MAN'S NEED AND GOD'S ACTION
THE CREATIVE YEARS
HEREIN IS LOVE
THE MIRACLE OF DIALOGUE
PARTNERS IN PREACHING

SURVIVAL PLUS

by Reuel L. Howe

THE SEABURY PRESS · NEW YORK

ACKNOWLEDGMENTS

Grateful acknowledgment is made to the following publishers for permission to use copyrighted material from the titles listed:

Detroit Free Press—Editorial, December 26, 1969. Copyright 1969 by Detroit Free Press.
Alfred A. Knopf, Inc.—Kahlil Gibran, *The Prophet.* Copyright 1923 by Kahlil Gibran; copyright renewed 1951 by Administrators C.T.A. of Kahlil Gibran Estate and Mary G. Gibran.
TIME, August 17, 1970—"When the Young Teach the Old to Learn." Copyright 1970 by Time Inc.
Scriptural quotations are from the *Revised Standard Version of the Bible, copyrighted* 1946 and 1952 by the Division of Christian Education, National Council of Churches.

To
Arthur R. Buckley,
editor and friend,
whose understanding, patience,
and skill
have contributed clarity
and readability
to my books

To the Reader

This book is written in response to the thousands of communications, written and verbal, from readers of *The Miracle of Dialogue* who have asked for an elaboration and further application of that theme to some of the conflicts, changes, and resulting ambiguities of our time.

It is written in response to the threat to human love and life resulting from prevalent disillusionment, and loss of faith in God, church, moral values, man, and in many of our political and economic institutions.

Some of the current "rebellions" are speaking truths that need to be heard. Can we hear them and respond? Can we see and comprehend? The despair that many thoughtful people feel about the present and the future is justified, but the same thoughtfulness is needed to see and hear the signs of promise and possibility which are essential if we are to move from despair to growth and achievement. Despair is response to things that have happened. Hope is living actively in anticipation of

viii To the Reader

viii To the Reader

things that have not yet happened. I write out of faith's struggle against a fermenting, creeping doubt that there is no future, a doubt that sometimes threatens to overwhelm us.

This book, therefore, is about survival and growth, about the struggle between life and death, between the creative powers of man and his power to destroy himself and others. We are concerned here with more than the survival of the individual. He cannot survive alone. Retreat into privacy, into preoccupation with our own well-being and safety, serves a uterine intention and is a reversal of the life process. To survive we will have to find a way to move out of our defensive selves, into the very complexity of the life that threatens us, with human resources that can free us to cope with the terrifying dehumanizing forces that are so technologically implemented.

Some say it is too late. Just at the time when we have achieved a mastery over nature, we become the slave of our own creation. We have or are acquiring all knowledge, we have achieved power and know-how for any task, but we do not have love and the ability to live with ourselves and others. Our future will depend upon our ability to make our decisions out of human values and to act and build on foundations of compassion and mutual interest.

Can we do it? With others I wonder! And yet in spite of discouragement and some despair, I was to find this book taking substance and form in my mind as I met with men and women and wrestled with the questions, doubts, and hopes that emerged out of their struggles as individuals and leaders. Yes, I believe we can do it; but courage and the willingness to grow and change will be required of us.

Some people die on the vine: they go on living but lose their aliveness. They become the walking dead. Others remain alive, they even grow, no matter how rough life is for them. Even if they are physically incapacitated, they retain their interests and their capacity to respond creatively. What explains this difference? Is there something that can be learned from such a study that would help us to choose life instead of death, that would keep our institutions and organizations reformingly and transformingly alive, changing and responsive to the vitality that they are meant to serve?

In this book I offer a principle that, in my experience, does enable us to live with our changes, conflicts, ambiguities, and questions of the present and the future.

I wish to thank my wife, Peggy, for assisting in the writing of the original manuscript, and Kay Riley for typing it; and Barbara Rexford for assisting in the editing and typing of the final manuscript. I am grateful to Mary Banks, my secretary, for assuming additional responsibilities so that I might work on my manuscript.

I must also acknowledge my indebtedness in Chapter 2 to Abraham Maslow's *Toward a Psychology of Being*; and in Chapters 8 and 9 to John M. Dorsey's *Growth of Self-Insight*.

R. L. H.

Contents

SURVIVAL PLUS

Man, the creature, who forms and transforms the creation, cannot create. But he, each man, can expose himself and others to the creative spirit.

—Martin Buber

1. Survival Demands Growth

Looking back over the last two decades, what we now see to have been the major factor in our lives is change—change of an all-pervasive kind which has touched and transformed every aspect and department of life, both personal and social.

The character of this change has been vastly different from the types of change which society had experienced in the past. It goes far beyond the old contradictory mixtures of good and evil; beyond the old conflicts arising from cultural trends and preferences; and beyond the old needs to reform or modernize institutions. What we now realize is that our accumulation of knowledge and technological capacity has been pushing us at breathtaking speed to new developments and complexities for which neither our education nor our experience has prepared us. Just as we used to assume that our environment was

inexhaustible, we also assumed that our powers of adapta-
bility to change were unlimited. Today we know differ-
ently. In his book *Future Shock*, Alvin Toffler has set
forth for us some of the disturbing dimensions of this
phenomenon: countless people are already exhausted
from the effort simply to survive.

The important psychological fact in all this for us is
that such accelerating change intensifies the strain that
we must bear and requires that we maintain a firm hold
on our sense of identity and an alert awareness of the
human resources which we have for adapting constructively to change.

Some Common Attitudes Toward Change

One major strand of our difficulties in handling change
lies, of course, in ourselves—that is, in our attitudes
toward change. When we examine some of these characteristic attitudes, we soon see how they inhibit us from
even beginning to grapple with the problems of change.
Thus empty and unfocused, we are quickly threatened
and easily destroyed.

What are some of the characteristic attitudes toward
change?

1. Some of us try to meet it by looking for a return to
an earlier time and condition. We long for the "good old
days" and for a "return to normal." We don't realize that
there can be no going back. We cannot even stay where
and as we are. If we are to grow, we must move forward,
with fear as well as courage, to a new day and a new
way of coping with the liveliness of the world.

2. Others of us may try to deal with the problems and
complexities of life by reducing them to some simple
solution. We jump on bandwagons and become eco-

nomic, political, or religious fundamentalists. We may strive for a sense of well-being by excluding what we cannot accept. We live lives of oversimplified reality which in the end turns out to be no reality at all.

3. A third self-defeating response is for us to deny that change is occurring. A common observation of parents to their children is that "history repeats itself." We look for continuities but cannot face and accept discontinuities, thus making ourselves more vulnerable to the time when massive change finally overtakes and overwhelms us.

4. Another way of dealing with the threat of change is for us to get lost in some part of the complexity. The development of specialization gives many specialists a way of retreating from their total responsibility, especially their responsibility to relate their specialty to others in the interests of correlation and cooperation. Instead, they contribute to the fragmentation of knowledge and endeavor, thus worsening the effect of change.

Denied by these attitudes any genuine adaptive means, people become confused, apathetic, irritable, violent, and unable to cope with the real and overwhelming issues facing them. Unable to face the challenges of today, they are unprepared to meet those of the future.

Areas of Conflict

Change is not the only ingredient in our disorientation. Because of both change itself and our characteristic attitudes toward it, sharp conflict and confrontations have also emerged. We are torn between accepting change at all, accepting it in some areas and not in others, or to one degree and not to another, or finally simply opting for total change. Each of us is a willing or unwilling participant in these conflicts and struggles, which we know deep in our hearts will decide to no small degree our future—personal, national, global.

Here again the areas of conflict span every aspect of our lives.

Man vs. Man. In this area, the major conflicts center upon the issues relating to race, sex, and generational differences. Among the sharpest of these issues are those touching on equality and equal opportunity for all, male-female relationship and the new roles of the sexes, and the alienation of youth and adult.

Man vs. Environment. The most frightening changes as sources of sharp conflict are occurring in relation to our environment. No longer can we take air, water, land, or mineral deposits for granted. The air we breathe is now dangerous to our health, and so dense that the light and warmth of the sun are impeded. Oceans, lakes, and streams are filthy with human and industrial waste. Unbridled technology and exploitation have poisoned the earth and are fast making it unfit for habitation. We now have to choose between the earth as a beautiful and healthful place to live and unrestrained dumping of waste, unlimited production, and selfish affluence as goals of living.

Men vs. Technology. In this area the development of cybernetics is changing the very concept of work around which so much of our lives and social relationships have been built. The full effect of this kind of change on motivation, style of living, and our resources cannot be fully anticipated. Most important have been the technological changes in the conduct of war, which have had a profound effect on our attitudes toward war itself. For centuries war has been accepted as a means for settling conflict. Today the development of massive weapons of total destruction has, in the minds of all thoughtful people, eliminated war as an available or viable solution to international conflict because neither side can win and all would be destroyed. New ways then simply must be found to settle these differences and new relationships developed if the human race is to survive.

The most depressing element in our conflicts as they relate both to ecology and technology is our inability to escape from the "scarcity" philosophy of our past and our contradictory belief in unlimited growth. The conditions of the past that generated these beliefs will never return: we have already compromised beyond reclaim the tenets of "scarcity" and have exhausted—or have come close to exhausting—the resources on which the concept of unlimited growth was built. As a measure for gauging success, Gross National Product is obsolete, and new values and means of measurement are needed to assess achievement: an alternative system to our present capitalistic, competitive economy devised for conditions long since changed. Many people think that scientists will give us the answers to our environmental and technological problems. Unfortunately for that hope, too many scientists have allowed themselves to become mesmerized by technological progress as an end in itself without reference to the basic needs of human fulfillment. The restraining voices heard from the realms of science have been few indeed.

Man vs. Education. The sharp conflicts that we have witnessed around the issues of objectives and process in education should eventually help us evolve a way of living that will enable us to actualize more fully our human potential. Some of the student dissent must be heard and responded to. Education has been serving the wrong purposes. We have accumulated such enormous amounts of knowledge that we require the assistance of computers to handle it, and we have developed a technology that makes it possible for man to do many things that only a few years ago would have been unbelievable. But we have not made anything like comparable progress in learning to live together; and relational development has failed to keep pace with our knowledge and technical progress. Without relational wisdom and competence, knowledge and technical skill become destructive monsters. Education, therefore, faces the difficult task of changing its motives, purposes, and processes, and of helping students of whatever age to prize human values and relations as primary, with knowledge and technology serving as resources and means toward fulfillment.

Man vs. the Institutional Church. People's suspicion and alienation from their institutions is both potential and real in every age. In our own time we are experiencing this alienation of people from the institutional church. Among the many causes is the tendency of the church as an institution to become preoccupied with its own image, programs, and success with diminishing concern for and capacity to express the faith it professes in relation to the changing and varying idioms, needs, and capacities of the people.

It may seek to maintain tradition and ignore contemporary questions; or it may involve itself in contemporary issues and abandon the living tradition that gave it birth. The institutional church often seeks to impose past theology and religious formulas and styles of life on people without regard for the meanings that are now motivating them. The ordained leadership of the church is often educated away from the possibilities of communication with the laity from whom they come and to whom they must return as clergy. Theology is studied as an end in itself and not in relation to the deep questions that individuals and society have. Religious observance is allowed to become formal and worship impersonal and only cerebral. Therefore, it becomes possible for people who believe in the "eternal" God to fear change; to talk about redemption but abhor inevitable and necessary conflict; to point to the resurrection but disguise and hide from the reality of death and fail to accept it as an indispensable part of life; to refer to Jesus as Saviour but because they hide from the reality of their sin to have no sense of need for a saviour.

The more the church becomes an end in itself, the less it is related to life and the more alienation it causes.

Conflict of Cultures

All these developments have, in a sense, merged to produce a conflict of cultures—the old and the new. In his book *The Pursuit of Loneliness*, Philip E. Slater contrasts these cultural viewpoints as follows: "The old culture, when forced to choose, tends to give preference to property rights over personal rights, technological requirements over human needs, competition over cooperation, violence over sexuality, concentration over distribution, the producer over the consumer, means over ends, secrecy over openness, social reforms over personal expression, striving over gratification, Oedipal love over communal love." The old and new cultures are empowered by opposite motives and cannot be reconciled. Dr. Slater identifies scarcity as the core of the old culture. People must compete for the limited resources: "Those who can take the largest share of the scarce resources are said to be 'successful.' "

The new culture is based on the assumption that important human needs are easily satisfied and that the resources for doing so are plentiful. "The only danger to humans is human aggression," Dr. Slater adds. "There is no reason outside of human perversity for peace not to reign and for life not to be spent in the cultivation of joy and beauty." He points out that the resources for the beautiful life are not as accessible as the new culture assumes because of the restraints the old culture has put on them.

The old culture is restrained, colorless, and tasteless in its emphasis on "good taste"; the new culture is responsive to stimulus, color, and taste. The new culture is storming the foundations of the old with "psychedelic colors, amplified sound, exotic books and films, bright and elaborate clothing, spicy food, intense words, angry and irreverent satire." The old culture is afraid of stimulus and the new culture shows signs of undersensitivity to stimuli.

Survival and Growth

What is to be our future if, caught in the midst of these conflicts, we are to avoid destruction by our very polarization?

First, we must grant that we have only limited control over what happens to us. We are always standing in a rain of happenings, some of which fall on us as blessings, others pelt us with tragic force. The answer to our human situation cannot be found in what befalls us but in the responses we give to what is happening to us. We shall be greatly helped if we do not approach life with naïve expectations and presuppositions. This is particularly true now.

Second, we need to clarify our understanding of what survival means. It does not mean any simplistic return to the past or a mere passive hanging onto life with ever narrowing spheres of interest and action. Survival, as we shall use the term, is a positive concept—something we do to renew our hold on life. It means acknowledging mistakes and making whatever changes are called for. It means achieving new awareness, integrity, and a sustaining core of values. And, above all, it means *growth*, finding the right way to use all our resources, human and material, and to deepen and expand our interpersonal relationships. In our present human situation without such growth we cannot survive in any meaningful way.

As I wrote in *The Miracle of Dialogue*, one indispensable tool for growth and survival is dialogue. Too many people think of dialogue as a verbal activity only, a misconception which renders dialogue powerless in the face of the tough situations that call for it. Dialogue requires an attitude and relationship of *inclusion* which provides the capacity for engaging in dialogue. It shall be our purpose in this book to explore, define, and apply the basic principle of this *inclusionism*, which is one means at our disposal for altering situations of polarization and for achieving growth in what would otherwise be destructive conflict.

Before examining *inclusionism* and its rival, exclusionism, we should first remind ourselves of the human resources that man has developed over the centuries on which to build his faith in the possibilities of reciprocal and constructive action and communication in times such as these.

2. Growth and Its Dynamics

In view of the personal and cultural crisis that we all face and its symptoms that we have just examined, the first question which should receive our attention is: What resources are available to us for meeting this crisis? In a general way, we may answer that most of the human resources which man has acquired and developed over the centuries of his evolution and history continue to be available to him in the present situation provided that he does not ignore them, but puts them to conscious use. Accordingly, in this chapter we shall investigate what some of these resources are and what the dynamics of man's growth have been.

Man's Resources for Growth

The first resource which we might mention is the centering, healing, and unifying quality of life found in biological man. The healing powers of our bodies are always present and at work. When our bodies are invaded by hostile organisms, they immediately begin to fight the enemy; and the symptoms of illness are the result of this battle against the enemy. If the body is healthy, a scratch on the hand is healed in a matter of days. We take the healing process so for granted that we fail to appreciate the miracle of healing. The physician does not heal us; he brings the skills and knowledge of the science of medicine to the aid of the body's own healing powers. When our bodies lose their power to heal, death is on the way, and there is little that medicine can do to prevent it.

The psyche, too, can be worn away by repeated disappointments and frustrations, and eventually break down or give up the struggle. There is nevertheless present in the psyche the same drive toward health and unity, the same force that moves toward healing, that is found in the body. In spite of problems of one kind or another, men have risen again and again to a belief in themselves, in others, and in the possibilities of the future. Man's survival powers can be amazing in the face of an adverse psychological and sociological environment. We have learned, furthermore, that we can release these powers of healing and unification in others through therapies and other forms of care. For example, the current human potential movement is built on this very principle and aims to call forth the resources for growth that exist within each person in his relationships with others.

Then there is to be observed the presence of a creative drive in man, which has been found in all cultures and among all peoples, from the most primitive. From the time that our remote ancestor picked up his first stick or bone fragment to use as a tool, man began to use his potential power of inventiveness that has developed over thousands of years into the production today of tools of unbelievable refinement. Along with this capacity has gone the human need to adorn and beautify everything that we make. Even man's earliest crude tools and utensils bear evidence of this desire to decorate and adorn. Again, when calamity has overtaken him and chaos sought to overwhelm him, he has always struggled to achieve order and organization and new purpose. There is something in man, in us all, that will not consent to destruction and death.

It is supportive to realize also that the world of nature operates in response to laws and rhythms. This orderly dependability of the structure of nature has made it possible for us to unravel some of the mysteries of the physical world: to discover the laws of matter and energy, to utilize these energies, and to transform them into useful powers. It is this stability in nature that has enabled man to utilize its laws and to build and guide his vehicles to the moon. Because of the laws inherent in creation, we learn to understand and heal diseases, to develop vast systems of communication and transportation, and to develop an industrial complex that is as bewildering in complexity as it is productive.

Equally important are the benign powers that operate between man and man. First of these is the love of one person for another. The prototype of human love is the force of mutual attraction between particles of energy and forms of life which, in the evolutionary process, came together in new forms and levels of life. Throughout the eons of evolution this centering and unifying energy of developing life manifested itself in higher and higher forms until finally it was capable of psychological and social expression of human love. Love as a centering and unifying force has always been a part of life, but it appears in man in unique form. Many of us now see it as the source and sustainer of life. We seek to identify with it, to share and respond to it. We have given this love all kinds of names, including "God." The question is: Can we be faithful to it? Can we respond so that it can be a focus for what we have to do in order to bring the work of creation to fulfillment? Can we accept the challenge as a part of God's creation?

We know how indispensable love is for the personal development of a child. Given food and all other care, but not love, the child will die, or simply wither and fail to develop as a person. The gift of love, in spite of all other deprivations, will bring a child through. He needs to be loved in order to love himself and therefore to be able to love others. As I pointed out in *Man's Need and God's Action*, a child needs love most when he is most unlovable, a principle that holds true not only for children but for adults, too. Love has the power to heal, to change the direction of a life that is in trouble. Love can also free us to be open to new life, new possibilities. Love can cause us to surrender our lives in an act of love for others. All of this is so obviously true and yet, tragically, is overlooked as a basis for living. Human living, to be sure, is a mixed experience. On the one hand, it is ego-centering, diverse and demonic; on the other hand, it is convergent, unifying and healing. Our difficulty seems to be that we are unable to maintain in life a unified awareness of these two capacities. Either we are cynical and without hope because of the disillusionment stemming from experience of the demonic, or we are sanguine and naïve because of expectations that are not balanced by a realization of the presence in us and others of the egocentric and demonic. To be human, therefore, means a variety of things. In times of disaster the National Guard has to be called out to keep some men from looting homes and stores, and the afflicted have to be protected from the unscrupulous who would sell food at exorbitant prices, exploiting the dire need of the victims.

In contrast, other kinds of people freely render personal service and give large sums of money in order to help the suffering. There are saints and sinners, creators of mediocrity and ugliness, and creators of greatness and beauty. There are tyrants and just men, mean men and heroic, defensive men and brave, status quoers and innovators, dependents and self-actualizers, followers and leaders. All are human. Obviously it is a state of being in which there is a variety of hazards and hopes. Yet in the beginning God created man and woman. We all have come from this same source of love and life. When people do not come together and interact, separation and alienation follow and ultimately produce only sickness and death. Interaction produces the flow of current, the surge of life. We are life, and life comes from life.

We are all both the same and different. We are the same in many ways. We all have heads in the same place, arms with like functions, legs attached to our torsos. We all have hair, eyes, ears, fingers, and toes. We all have to breathe and eat to live, and to eliminate and bathe to stay healthy. All these characteristics and many more we have in common.

There are also, however, a number of differences that distinguish us from each other. Happily, there are those of sex that keep us intrigued, fulfilled, and frustrated. Sadly, there is the demon of skin color, a difference that men have turned into a nightmare of divisiveness. There are also differences of facial structure and expression, differences of hair and eye color, shape of ears, nose and chin, and differences of posture and movement which lend variety to appearance and movement. No two of us are exactly alike. This is borne out most dramatically by the uniqueness of our fingerprints, which are infinitely different. Thus it can be said that while every person is the same in many ways, in the final analysis each is unique.

Differences are also to be noted in our responses to what happens to us. In some respects our responses are the same: threats give rise to fear and defensiveness; good fortune produces pleasure and fulfillment. In other respects our individual responses will differ: one person's response to fear will be to remain defensive, while another will undertake to deal realistically and constructively with it.

Furthermore, our sameness is both a liability and a resource. Our sameness can at times be reassuring. It is good to know, for example, that we are like other people and they are like us; to discover the opposite to be true would alarm us. It is good to know that since growth is painful for us, it is for others also. We find comforting the knowledge that all men know fear and need love. And yet, on the negative side, the reassurance of sameness and our need of it can turn us into nonthinking conformists seeking womblike security.

Our uniqueness is also a liability and a resource. We can want to be different for the sake of being different; or our need for uniqueness may make us unaccepting of sameness. It can become a basis for snobbism and elitism. On the positive side, however, the development of uniqueness can lead to experimentation, innovation, new life styles, and exciting variations of point of view.

Growth As a Creative Force

How can we build creatively on our sameness and at the same time not lose our uniqueness? The answer is to be found in maintaining our capacity for growth. Evolution is a process of growth; growth is a characteristic of nature; and the resources of growth are built into every individual who is born. The same is true for or-

ganizations. Consolidation and exploitation of resources
are a poor substitute for growth. The crises of life occur
when we seek to secure what we have and give up the
open adventure of growth itself.

The kind of growth about which we are talking, the
kind that alone can ensure survival, is personal growth:
growth of talents, of relationships, of love, of a capacity
to see and hear more deeply the meanings of life. The
capacity to give and to receive graciously, the capacity
to sort out the tinsel from the gold of human experience,
the capacity to think and feel, to distinguish the real
and congruent in words and actions. Growth in these
directions changes individuals and organizations and can
free religion, government, education, and our culture for
more courageous and competent action. Much of the
anguish and tragedy of human life is caused by the
determination to "play it safe" with the result that the
defensive person or organization slowly dies. The hope
of life is maintained when man continues to grow and
maintain his capacity for openness.

Growth in the beginning of an individual's life is
unconscious and automatic. The power to develop and
grow is built into the individual and favored and stimulated by his environment. The first development takes
place in his mother's womb: the uniting of the two
cells is followed by an intricate process of unfolding,
until finally there emerges a fully formed man-child,
possessing, if there have been no accidents, all the external features and characteristics needed for living.

Outside the womb the infant's life unconsciously and
automatically proceeds; although he has to be slapped to
begin breathing, the process, once begun, continues without his choosing. Quite naturally and without effort on
his part, various growth stages succeed one another. He
begins to be able to focus his eyes, to reach out and

grasp things, to move them from one place to another, to make sounds that in a primitive way control the movements and actions of others, to smile and respond, to sit up, crawl, stand, and finally to walk. Each one of these experiences is a growth frontier for him. With each one he experiences satisfaction and joy, and knows the pleasure and approval of the important people around him at each new achievement.

With each such movement forward, however, the child experiences a backward pull to the security and comfort of his previous state of well-being. Life on a growth frontier can be frightening after a while, and a brief period of retreat is needed for the sake of reassurance and rest. There is risk involved in maintaining a position on the frontier, so that a time of security in a previous state of being is necessary for the health of the individual. An interesting example of this to-and-fro movement can be seen when the child learns to walk. His delight in his new ability is unmistakable, and he naturally basks in the admiration of those around him. After a time, however, he may refuse to walk and want to be carried. This retreat to his former state of security is as much a part of growth as was the forward movement. The advance and the withdrawal must go together. Hopefully the withdrawal will be followed by another advance. After being carried for a while, the child resumes walking and gradually extends the areas of his travels. Usually in the early years of life this rhythm of growth and retreat continues quite automatically as long as the environment, personal and otherwise, is encouraging and supportive.

Growth vs. Retreat

There are two sets of forces at work here: the growth and retreat forces within the individual; and the growth and retreat forces operating in his environment. Fortunate is the child who has parents and teachers who have some belief in him during the times when he needs to withdraw and experience again the more primitive security. Such a child has a maximum chance of being able to continue to grow during the whole course of his life.

Sad, however, is the plight of the child whose personal and physical environment is not encouraging to his growth attempts and fails to give him support during his adverse experiences. In the first instance the encouragement of adults, parents and teachers especially, joins with the growth forces in the child to keep him moving ahead. In the second instance, condemnation or hostility toward his withdrawal needs tends to divert him from new growth possibilities and encourage him to settle for the kind of security in which the amount of risk is minimal. Critical, unaccepting parents and teachers strengthen the conservative, defensive forces in the child. If he has experienced too much nonacceptance and been deprived of his basic need for love and encouragement, he accumulates such a body of need that he is not free to grow. Most of his decisions, conscious and unconscious, will be for safety and the preservation of things as they are. During childhood the growth forces within a child are strong, and given half a chance, he moves forward spontaneously, joyously, freely, excitingly, and with a wonderful sense of possibility. Long before the individual reaches his teens, however, a change takes place. More and more he is faced with the necessity of evaluating his purposes, deciding what is important to him, and acting in response to what feels good to him. At this point growth ceases to be automatic and becomes a matter of individual decision, and he may decide against growth and for security, a primitive uterine kind of security; or he may choose to risk the dangers of growth.

This pattern is true of adults also. There are forces in us that pull us back to what we knew in the past as satisfying, safe, and secure. We are afraid to risk what we have for the sake of the future, for the sake of an unknown good. We do not want to be different from others, to stand alone. If so, most of our life decisions are made in the interests of security and against change. We cannot return to the womb from which we came, and so out of our religion, our convictions, our prejudices, our fears and our hatreds, we build new shelters in which to hide.

On the other hand, our openness to growth may move us out to new frontiers, to the discovery of new powers and capacities. We can feel free to take risks, and invest ourselves in new relationships and enterprises that will bring personal and social capital gains as well as dividends. Instead of being status quoers, we become self-actualizers, innovators, creative persons; instead of running from the world, we face it with confidence even though we may sometimes be afraid. The conflict between these retreat and growth patterns is a deep-seated part of our nature. Each of us, both within and without, feels pulled both ways by it. Yet we were born both *to be* and *to become*.

As we grow older, beginning shortly after puberty, growth is less determined by natural unfolding and more by the individual's own decisions, either to risk the possibilities of growth or to choose securities already achieved. The grower faces his fear to risk, accepts the pain and dangers in growing for the sake of satisfactions to be achieved; and knows that the death or abandonment of present good is often the doorway to future good and new life. The status quoer decides against the inevitable risks of growth and chooses a way of life that leads to his own diminishment and gradual personal

death. The status quoer chooses a death that leads nowhere; the grower chooses a death that leads to more life.

This issue of growth vs. death is as true for institutions
and organizations as it is for individuals. Every organization may also evaluate its life in terms of its movement
forward or backward, toward growth or toward death.

Abraham Maslow, in his book *Toward a Psychology
of Being,* has provided two very useful concepts for
understanding this conflict and the two kinds of security:
he distinguishes between *deficiency need* and *growth
need.*

What is meant by deficiency need? These are the
kinds of needs which if satisfied keep us from growing:
for example, our need for approval in everything that
we do; our inability to accept criticism as a source of
learning; our need to be right, which alienates us from
other people; or our need to control. Many of our fears
are deficiency needs. All of these, because of our preoccupation with them and our tendency to minister to
them, keep us from growing. We become self-protective,
defensive people; we think of security as something to
hoard, to accumulate. Speaking figuratively, such people
hide their security under the mattress of their psyche
because they are afraid to invest it. Personally and
socially, they become status quoers who seek for themselves positions in life of low risk and high safety.

In contrast, there are the growth needs: the need to
have new experiences, to achieve new relationships, to
take risks for the sake of possible future good, the need
to give, to love, to make sacrifices, to learn new things,
to acquire new skills, to explore the potentialities of one's
self, others, and the world in which one lives. To these
people security is not something to hoard but to spend.
Already secure in themselves, they are free to invest themselves for the sake of growth and its rewards. Whatever

of risk is involved is external and not ego-related in a destructive way. They are able to trust and to stimulate trust in others.

The Purposes of Growth

We cannot, however, discuss growth without determining what are its purposes and satisfactions. We have already noted that the goals and forms of our religious, political, economic, and social life are not changing as rapidly as the challenges to them seem to demand. The old forms are not equal to the new tasks, and the individuals exclusively dedicated to those forms have such a heavy investment in their dubious values that they are unwilling to consider changes that seem necessary. We have seen that our knowledge and technology alone cannot save us; it has become apparent and has been witnessed to by young and old alike that we need a relational basis in order to utilize creatively our accumulations of knowledge and technology. To achieve this, enterprises need to be centered in the unifying concern for the personal, individually and corporately. All our institutions need the focus of the relational.

In order to achieve more of the relational, we need individuals and organizations that have the following capacities. First, we need persons who are self-affirming, who take delight in the realization that they are growing persons. We need people who know the joy of being; who at different periods in their life can say, "I am who I am" with increasing meaning. They will be able to love others and require only a minimal return of love for themselves and the maintenance of their own ego and being. Their growth needs will steadily increase while their deficiency needs decrease. Their motives, decisions, and actions will be outward and generous.

Second, we need persons in this new society whose growth motive is to have a sense of joy in and love for others. Their joy will lie in their being in a relation, and their capacity to give to others will be their fulfillment and the reward of their love. They will be open to others rather than try to confine others to some image of their choosing.

Third, we need people who will have a sense of interest and wonder in the world in which they live and take satisfaction in learning the skills for living in it. They will delight to explore the unknown and mysterious, to look for new areas in which they can become interested. Their greatest fear is the fear of not growing, the fear of being cut off from possibilities of new relationships to their expanding world.

Fourth, we need persons for this time of change whose growth has been such that they can freely correlate old and satisfying experiences with new and challenging ones. Their special contribution will be to help us to merge the old with the new and to construct the new institutional forms that are so desperately needed.

Fifth, we also need leaders whose growth has enabled them to develop criteria for electing, with openness and competence, a way of life. They will not be swayed by the wishes and selfish demands of others; rather, out of the integrity of their own being and their appreciation of the being of others, they will make their choices in the interests of mutual becoming.

Sixth, finally we need people who will be responsive out of the exigencies and changes of life to the pole star of love and the community of men that only love can build, and upon which now, in the time of transition, the future of human life depends.

Yes, we need such people. But how is growth in these capacities to be achieved?

3. Two Opposing Life Principles

Our life situation today, it is generally agreed, is such that if we are going to have a future, we must begin now to decide and act on its behalf. The crucial question, then, which we must undertake to explore asks: Is there a principle of living which can help us out of the present morass of despair, on the one side, and polarization, on the other? Is there a principle which, applied to our lives, can bring us out of our despair, shock, or defensiveness, encourage us in patterns of growth, and prepare us for survival at a new and higher level of human living?

It is my observation that people tend, in the main, to approach and organize their lives around one or the other of two principles. In one case the approach and organization, if not unconscious, is at least unexamined because it is motivated by fear and deep psychic needs of defensiveness. In the other case, the approach and organization to life is freely chosen, and quite consciously developed and appraised. Things don't just happen; situations are met, their challenges responded to, and the possibilities of human life seized and developed. We have named the former (and negative) principle *exclusionism*; the latter and positive one we shall call *inclusionism*.

In this chapter we shall examine and contrast these principles in some detail, giving major attention to the principle of inclusion. In fact, the remainder of the book will undertake to analyze the dynamics and process of the principle and to apply it to a number of important life situations. For it is my conviction that the application of the principle of inclusion has accomplished the miraculous human transformations in man's history; and that we ourselves shall have a future only to the degree that we practice this principle in all we do.

The Exclusionist Principle

The principle of exclusion, as we have noted, is that principle of living which, I believe, is implicit in defensiveness, status quoism, and womb-building. The exclusionist is on guard against anything new or different in the way of people, styles of life, values, ideas, programs, or organizations. He is antilife because he is afraid. Thus all of his relationships are defensive. He has an inordinate need to be right. He cannot tolerate imperfection in others, in those who are close to him, and most of all, in himself. He is unable to cope with mistakes and errors. His relationships, for the most part, are alienated ones, whether they be with the members of his immediate family, his colleagues, his friends. Likewise, his relationship with whatever god he serves is hostile and dated.

He sharply categorizes and separates things and people into those he likes and those he does not like. His convictions have turned into prejudices, his communication is monological, he is not accessible to the meanings of others, but is aggressive in presenting *his* meanings to others. The categories by which he condemns and judges people increase the older he grows. He likes less and less, he responds to less and less, his interests become more narrow and self-centered, his prejudices increase, his gods get smaller and smaller, and his soul becomes increasingly incapable of feeling and expressing compassion.

The exclusionist looks to the past for reassurance. He dodges the tasks of the present and refuses to look at the challenges of the future. He wants the old times to return because they were the best, and yet his evaluation of the past is superficial and incomplete. He sees only what he wants to see; his tolerances are minimal. He has become a hideous caricature of the child that he once was, and a denial of all the potentialities that once existed in that child.

What is excluded by the exclusionist? He rejects people, especially those of a different race or religion, people who have succeeded or who have creative and strong personalities. He rejects new ideas, values, and experiences that he cannot instantly accommodate, and such issues and problems that challenge or seem to threaten him; open housing, for example, might be such an issue.

The greatest pitfall of the exclusionist is that in setting himself up as a judge of other people and events, he automatically excludes their participation in any way in his life and excludes himself from their enterprises. He is not free to include himself in the frame of others' creative thinking and working, and seeks only to maintain his own defensive identity. By his exclusionism and failure to interact with others, he receives no new data or insights that might give him perspective on himself. Without such feedback he lacks the means to his own possible growth. The exclusionist wants to remain as he is, and as the poet Rilke writes, "That which would remain what it is renounces existence."

An exclusionist falls prey to all kinds of illusions: illusions of omnipotence, perfectibility, rightness and importance, no one of which is substantiated by his reality situation. For example, an exclusionist was heard to say in relation to the raising of his children, "If I had it to do over again, I would not change a single concept or method"—a horrendous admission that he had learned nothing from the experience of being a parent. The maintenance of such illusions consumes enormous amounts of defensive energy that might better be spent elsewhere. This particular self-righteous parent insisted on maintaining his illusion of rightness despite the evidence that his parental concepts and methods had produced disastrous results in his children.

Illusions of self-superiority often cause the exclusionist to rate himself higher than is warranted because of the inferior unrealistic standards he uses. Acceptance of his limitations would free him to explore the more realistic possibilities in and for himself. Even the healthy convictions of a man who is by principle exclusionist deteriorate into prejudices. The final result of a life of exclusion is usually rigid attitudes, dogmatic opinions, bitterness, hostility, and separation; in short, a living death. People who defensively live their lives by the principle of exclusionism spend their declining years in bitterness, not only unhappy with themselves, but creating unhappiness for all around them. They create a class of citizens known as the living dead, living but unburied!

Where do we find the exclusionists? They can be

found in every institution and organization; they can be identified by their insistence on looking solely to the past for their clues as they walk backward into history. Churches are favorite places for them. They use God, and the faith, their hymns, prayers, and good works, to build walls behind which they can hide from the challenges of the true kingdom of God and man. There they become doctrinally opinionated purveyors of a sterile and unrenewed tradition, judgmental and lacking in any feeling of grace, either received or given.

This is a severely judgmental appraisal of exclusionists, but it is meant to be, because the principle by which they live has placed them in an outer darkness where they hear only their own weeping and wailing. And yet, because they are active and militant in their own defensiveness, ready to drag others into the same pattern of destructiveness, it is important that resistance to their defensiveness and destructiveness be made here with courage and vigor.

The Inclusionist Principle

The opposite principle to exclusion is inclusion. Instead of being on guard and closed to new people, new things, new values, new ideas—change of all kind—the inclusionist is open to them and gives them consideration. He is interested in the new possibilities that exist about him. This does not mean that he is like a blotter that soaks up everything with which it comes in contact. The inclusionist has his values, too, his convictions, and his philosophy of life, and believes that life has continuity as well as discontinuity. He respects the tradition that produced him even as he evaluates it. He wants his inclusion of tradition to renew it by making it a basis for a free, yet disciplined exploration of future possibilities.

He approaches experience from the strength of his own growing point of view, and he does not regard it as finished and closed. He is still building, looking for new materials, new styles that he can incorporate into the genius of his own creation. He is prepared to accept what he can accept in the way of additions to his own maturing philosophy and life style, and is capable of dispassionately excluding that which for the moment is contradictory to the structure he is building. He may even for the moment exclude values which he will later include.

So we see that exclusion is a necessary part of inclusion, but there is an important difference between the exclusion of the exclusionist and the exclusion of the inclusionist. In the first instance, exclusion is an unexamined way of life. In the case of the inclusionist, exclusion is a matter of nondefensive evaluation and decision, subject to continuing re-examination. Thus the inclusionist is a more trustworthy person than the exclusionist, and a more likely architect of the future.

An inclusionist is inevitably a growing person, because he is fed by so many sources from outside himself. Not only does he have structure for his living, but that structure, through the practice of inclusion, is kept flexible and adaptable to the changes in the life around him. If he encounters rigidities within himself, he is able to examine them dispassionately and determine what he needs to do in order to become more authentic and less compulsive at those points.

Only the inclusive person can be an authentic person because he has his own center of being, held openly in relation to the centers of others. Having integrity and being authentic is not a solo business, nor can growth be accomplished in isolation. Inclusion provides the basic stance that makes achievement of integrity, authenticity, and growth possible.

The following incident will perhaps serve to illustrate what we have been discussing. Several years ago two men were discussing the hippie movement. One of them said that the hippies were a disgrace to the human race and a danger to public health and decency, and wrote them off as a complete liability. Obviously his attitude was one of exclusion. The other man said that he found it difficult to accept their style of dress, their way of life, but that beneath all of the surface things that he could not approve, he saw that they were representing meanings that were important for people to hear. While he did not approve their way of making their witness, he nevertheless responded to their emphasis on love, community, and their challenge to the technological exploitation of nature and man. In another case, in handing down a decision in relation to violence on a campus, a judge spoke inclusively in relation to the right of anyone to hold any opinion and the freedom to express it wherever he could, but he denied them the right to act in ways that would interfere with the freedoms of others and threaten their safety. In the latter part of his statement, he was practicing the exclusion of an inclusionist.

Inclusion is the only way in which one can achieve wholeness. No one can be whole by himself. My meanings are all that I have, but I do not have the whole meaning about anything. But when I seek to include your meanings in my meanings, and you seek to include my meanings in yours, we each have taken a step toward wholeness. By mutually supplementing our meanings, we stand together in a fuller relation to the truth than we can possibly achieve separately.

There are many illustrations of this truth. Man needs woman in order to be whole, including the differences between them which can be a source of friction and alienation. Woman is incomplete without man, again including the anatomical, physical, and psychological differences. What constitutes manhood needs what constitutes womanhood if each is to be complete and whole. Marriages fail because differences are excluded and become sources of frustration and separation. Inclusion accomplishes union of differences as well as of congenialities. Through the practice of inclusion, a husband and wife with widely differing interests can effect a union that is richer because of the differences.

Again, the meaning of white must include the meaning of black, and black must include the meaning of white. Exclusionism on either side produces racism. If we are to find the solution to the race question, it will be through the practice of the principle of inclusion. And so it is with all our polarities: Protestantism—and denominationalism—without the Catholic principle of the universal church of all men for all times and all places, becomes divergent and exclusionist; and the Catholic, without the Protestant principle of individual conscience and the right of protest, becomes authoritarian and destructive of individual growth. So too, the positive must include the negative. Living must include dying. Love must include hostility. Joy must include sadness. Strength must include weakness. The exercise of power must include passivity. And any attempt to separate these in order to have one without the other is to rob life of some of its meaning. Many are trying now to use freedom exclusive of discipline, with the terrifying result that they are creating situations in which freedom is being destroyed for them as well as for others.

What Is to Be Included?

Some understanding of what constitutes the categories or subject matter of inclusion will help our growth in the practice of inclusion. The first category of inclusion, and one of primary importance, is the category of the self. Inclusionists are responsive to and responsible for themselves. They are also responsive to others. Many people are unfulfilled and frustrated because they cannot be real and congruent in relation to both themselves and others and are thus limited participants in human relations. A person who complains about the way other people treat him may be projecting his own lack of regard for himself. It seems to him that they do not include him, because he does not include himself.

One needs an open mind about who one is and what one can do in order to meet life, which is both a mystery and a promise. At the beginning of every conference at our Institute, as a part of the introductory evening, we ask each person to stand and to say, "I am who I am, and my name is Bill Jones." It is interesting to listen to the different ways in which people speak that formula and give their names. A few can say it with healthy assurance and eagerness. Some say it aggressively and arrogantly. Others say it timidly; some with embarrassment. Only a few are able matter-of-factly to include themselves in the conference by this means. The others obviously cannot; the introductory formula reveals how much they need to be included before they can learn to be self-inclusive. "I am who I am" is both an affirmation and a question. It affirms what has been actualized, and is a prayer for that which has not yet happened. And fortunate is the person who can be open to the not-yet-happened part of himself. The person with a closed identity shuts himself off from any revelation in life that seeks him out, and from a realization of the promise of his life that is possible.

Inclusion of oneself means accepting oneself as the resource of one's own becoming. It means awareness not only of one's problems but also of one's assets. When I ask a group of people to identify their problems, they are usually able to do so fairly freely and without much embarrassment. But when I ask them to identify their assets or resources, they experience real difficulty. In the first place, they are not used to thinking about themselves as having resources, and it may take some time before they discover that they have any, and what they are. The other difficulty is that they are too embarrassed to say anything positive about themselves. For example, one man had no trouble at all in identifying some of the areas of his inadequacy, but it took him a long time to realize and then to state that he possessed the important resource of being able to meet creatively almost any kind of event that happened in his life; and that in spite of certain inadequacies, he had this kind of confidence in himself. When questioned about his embarrassment in making this statement, he said he felt that people might think that he was bragging. Of course, in this situation, the man was not only criticizing himself, but the social attitudes in which we all have to live. It is true, of course, that self-affirmations can be corrupted by the demonic tendencies in our human nature. Self-confidence can easily deteriorate into arrogant self-assurance and conceit, "thinking of ourselves better than we ought to think."

Another act of inclusion of oneself is as a participant in every aspect of the human enterprise that becomes available to us. We are often tempted not to include ourselves. A young minister who had taken a courageous stand before his congregation on the issue of race relations in the community was severely criticized by the editor of the local newspaper in an editorial in which it was recommended that he leave social matters alone and stick to the Scriptures. The young minister's first response was one of anger and resentment; and he was tempted to write a scathing letter to the editor. He finally decided, however, to visit the editor and explain what he was trying to accomplish and from what motives, as well as to hear and understand the editor's point of view. Apparently the meeting produced a change. The editor wrote a second editorial in which he supported the minister; and the young minister also made a statement from the pulpit in which he provided a basis for understanding the editorials. The minister, in this case, was first tempted to exclude himself from the situation by venting his frustration and anger; had he followed this course he would have made the other part of himself unavailable to either the editor or the community. Instead, he included himself; rather than run away, he went to the editor, made himself available, and dealt with the issue that had been created, with the result that alienation and divergence were avoided. Thus a unification and centering of creative forces were brought about. Such is the work of inclusion. Had the minister succumbed to his exclusionist tendencies, he would have had an unhappy memory for the rest of his life. But by responding in an inclusionist way, he created a relationship that will be a source of strength and courage to him for the rest of his days. In sum, the exclusion of ourselves diminishes our own opportunities and those of others; whereas the inclusion of ourselves increases the possibilities of both. Many human relations would be greatly strengthened and improved if the participants could be more inclusive of who they are, of their thoughts and feelings, their words and actions. Many marriages are wrecked or fail because one of the partners is timid or defensive about who he or she is. The beginning of any relationship is to include who and what I am with the open expectation of having, very probably, to grow and change as the result of the personal interactions which ensue.

The second category of inclusion is the relational and naturally accompanies the act of self-inclusion. The minister in our story, in including himself in relation to the editor, included the editor as a part of the situation. In doing so, he had to listen and hear what the editor had to say from his side. The inclusionist always knows there are two sides to every issue or situation. The exclusionist, whether he excludes himself or others, tries to pretend that there is only one side, and therefore falsifies the relationship and its meaning. The inclusion of others is a source of new perspective, helps complete meaning, and contributes to the affirmation of the being of both.

The inclusion of others also means including what they do, which often is far from acceptable. The riot in Detroit in 1967 is instructive on this point. It could be interpreted as an act of inclusion on the part of the blacks, who, having been driven to desperation by the exclusionist activities of the community, resorted to violence in an attempt to include themselves in the only way they knew how. The riot, however, had a disastrous effect on them, on the community, and on the city because it was experienced by others as an act of exclusion. (That was not surprising, since desperate acts of inclusion are often experienced as exclusion.) It was imperative, then, that the community, or some part of it capable of doing so, understand and respond in an inclusive way to the riot, the rioters, and the meanings they expressed. Such a task was not easy, and not all efforts in that direction were effective. But whatever headway has been made has been the achievement of inclusion, not exclusion.

A religious meaning is available to us here. The whole

of Jesus' life was an act of inclusion. Whereas many of
the religious people of his time were setting up categories
by which to exclude others, he included these people. He
not only included them, but affirmed them and led them
from where they were to where they would be. The only
people he excluded were the excluders: those whose lack
of faith caused him to shake the dust of that place off
his feet—the Pharisees, money-changers in the temple,
and others. Finally, however, his life ended in a death
which he offered in behalf of all men, an act of inclusion
extended even to those who excluded him. As a result
of this inclusion, there was manifest on the face of the
earth a power for living that cannot be measured, and
which as yet has not been explored. The inclusionist, by
whatever name he calls himself, is a follower of that man
who first included himself in life and then included those
whom he had excluded and who had excluded him.

A third category of inclusion is the world, particularly what we think of as our environment. The story of
creation describes God as giving man dominion over all
things: "Then God said, 'Let us make man in our image,
after our likeness, and let him have dominion over the
fish of the sea and over the birds of the air and over
cattle and over all the earth, and over every creeping
thing that creeps upon the earth.' . . . And God said
to them, 'Be fruitful and multiply and fill the earth and
subdue it.' " Our environmental plight today shows how
irresponsibly and selfishly we have exercised that dominion. We have lived exclusively in relation to our environment, and in so doing, have almost destroyed it. Now,
with little margin available for remedial action, we need
to establish an inclusive relational view toward nature
and our environment. Pollution, noise, ugliness, and
steady deterioration of our living space are not inevitable.
They are the products of an engineering mentality,

which when not in dialogue with philosophical, social, and ecological values is exclusionist. Our technology must be brought into dialogue with the human values without which technology is destructive of human life. The same dogged technocratic narrow-mindedness that made this country affluent has long been at work wrecking it. Technology, uncorrelated with human relational values, is a demon against which man himself and his environment are defenseless.

Inclusion must also establish a fruitful relation between the meanings of tradition and those of contemporary life. Many of the present conflicts between tradition and the contemporary are unnecessary and simply show that we are thinking exclusively. Those who would exclude the insights of tradition as they try to wrestle with contemporary issues are depriving themselves of the important categories of continuity and context. Traditionalists, on the other hand, who exclude the questions and challenges that emerge out of the contemporary milieu dishonor the tradition which they profess to uphold and value. The inclusionist knows that he needs the roots and perspective of tradition to deal in an informed way with contemporary questions. He realizes that the forms in which tradition has come to us may have to change, but an inclusionist also is willing to admit that every form has built into it its own death, that his first loyalty is to what is vital in the content and perspective of the tradition. He further believes that if the form is kept in tension with this vitality, it may well be reformed, transformed, or replaced by a new form; and that such development is normal for the movement of life from one level of being to another.

The inclusionist also looks for changes in the relationships within and between organizations, whereas the exclusionist tends to cling to existing organizations, thus creating a condition in which new competing organizations have to be formed in order to accomplish new tasks. This is one of the major problems of contemporary government, which is so overburdened and overfinanced because bureaucratic committees, commissions, departments, and organizations have become obsolete and yet continue to exist and demand financial outlay. Furthermore, there is the waste of duplication, the unwieldiness that defeats decisive action, the development of government for government's sake, and a consequent ignoring of responsibilities for those it is supposed to represent. Instead, we have a condition of special and divergent interests that block the centering and the unification of resources for which the country is crying desperately. What is needed are more inclusionists in government. We need to choose statesmen rather than politicians, since the latter are responsive mostly to the pressures of special interests, whereas the former are rooted in the past, active in the present, but building for the future.

When it comes to matters of church and religion, the inclusionist is ecumenist. Attitudes based on exclusion have fragmented the Christian church and produced the scandal of denominationalism. Even though the movement for church unity is strong and growing, the exclusionist movement is also strong, because with every unification there is always a splinter group that will not go along with the reunion. The inclusionist thinks not only in terms of the relationship between the divided bodies within the Christian faith, but also in terms of the complementary relation of all religions, of a new and more inclusive ecumenism, from which might come power that would help the centering and unifying powers of mankind. The exclusionism of religions has contributed to the fragmentation of mankind.

Responsible Inclusionism

Inclusionists must assume responsibility for the results of their practice of inclusion. When men undertake to include each other, their responses, and the process of achieving a complementary relationship, they experience both positive and negative responses. Most people tend to welcome the positive and shun the negative. The inclusionist, however, will accept everything that happens as a source of learning, whereas the exclusionist accepts only what he likes, and tends to speak and act in ways that guarantee the responses he wants. The inclusionist believes that the achievement of relationship is worth any cost; therefore he is prepared to try to deal in an open way with whatever happens in the processes of relationship.

One of the most common responses that men experience when they undertake the act of inclusion is fear. There is the fear of what others may do in response, and there is the fear that they experience for and within themselves; and the fear of this fear will keep them from dealing with it. But an inclusionist will be willing to accept the negative as a part of the agenda of the situation. Where there is fear, of course, one inevitable response will be a conscious or unconscious hostility. The inclusionist is willing to face the fact of his own hostility and also accept the hostility of others as a normal component of human relations. The exclusionist, on his part, however, will pretend that he is not hostile.

Misunderstanding is another common characteristic of the attempt of human beings to live together. It is inevitable because I hear and interpret another's point of view in the terms of my own, which, of course, distorts the meanings that the other is trying to convey. The exclusionist responds to this situation by the defensive need to be right, which in the case of a misunderstanding means that the other person must be wrong. The inclusionist, on the other hand, will be open to having his understanding and interpretation of another's meanings corrected. He is prepared to have his understanding of the situation and viewpoint broaden and grow. Unlike the exclusionist, he would rather be in relation than be right.

Another concomitant of the practice of inclusion is the occurrence of doubt. In their dealings with one another, men will betray, disappoint, and disillusion each other, and from this develop mistrust, doubt, cynicism, and despair, which can grow to such proportions that the participants lose the power to believe and to trust altogether. In such cases, the exclusionist becomes despondent and without hope; the inclusionist, on the other hand, while he may be realistically aware of the situation, continues to act in anticipation of that which has not yet happened. This is what is meant by his act of faith and hope; and his offering of this kind of life attitude is an act of love. Since we are living in a time of much cynicism and despondency about men and their institutions, it is imperative that we seriously undertake the practice of inclusion, for it is the one means available to us for remaining open to the possibilities of things to come and thereby growing and surviving.

4. The Window of Awareness

In order to apply and practice the principle of inclusion, it is important that we understand the dynamics of awareness and how positively to deal with the negative aspects of our experiences. This chapter, therefore, will be devoted to an analysis of awareness, its relation to the principle of inclusion, and its function with respect to growth and survival.

Awareness, basically, is sensitivity to the potentiality of experience and the meanings that surround us and hammer at the door of consciousness. It is a sensitivity to both the positive and the negative elements in experience. It accepts the total content as subject matter for understanding and growth. A friend who was hurt and disillusioned by the failure of the organization he served said, in commenting about it: "I want to turn the experience into one of opportunity, of *kairos*." Hostility tells the aware person that someone is hurting and needs help; an expression of fear calls for his love and reassurance. He sees truth where other men see only confusion. Behind the world of appearances is the greater world of reality that can be seen only by the eyes of awareness.

If one is inclusionist, the beloved is a mystery whose nature and capacities he patiently explores and appreciates. Awareness of the beloved grows and taxes the powers of his love to respond worthily. Nothing is taken for granted, and every expression of love is a gift that has a breathtaking quality to it. Thus awareness is the window through which he sees the wonder, beauty, pathos, and meaning of the natural world and human relations.

Such awareness is not easily achieved or easily maintained because the "gravitational" pull of inattention and boredom is also steady and powerful. Effort is needed to keep the senses at work and to sustain focused attention and active reflection. I work in a place of exceeding beauty, and yet easily lose the sense of what passes before my eyes if I do not practice awareness.

Once in a while after some peak experience, we say with meaning, "It is good to be alive." At other times when we have encountered only difficulties, we still can say, "It was good for me in spite of the pain." The preparation for and cultivation of such experiences is the work of awareness and can be a source of real growth.

Training for Awareness

Awareness is the opposite of insensitivity and the kind of blurred vision that sees only sterility when actually there exist genuine possibilities for creativity. Awareness also destroys the boredom that is the result of our unfocused consciousness in thinking, feeling, and acting. Then too, awareness releases energy, whereas inattention or absentmindedness locks it up and is the first step in a process of repression. Eventually the avoidance of awareness causes unexpressed feeling to disturb bodily functioning and even structure. Twisted bodily positions are often expressions of repressed feelings just as difficulties in relationship can impair breathing.

How do we train ourselves for awareness? The first requirement is a sensitivity and openness to relationships. How easy it is to be so blinded by self-preoccupation that we are unable to discern the context of our ego design! How possible it is to live an entire day, even long periods of time, without being aware of the meanings that surround us and await to be recognized and incorporated in our lives. The relationships about which we are talking may include nature, people, events, issues, movements, sounds, tastes, odors, sights. Awareness of the networks of these relationships and their potentialities for our becoming is indispensable for growth and survival.

Consciousness that these relationships change and change us is important. They are not static like the lines of a diagram, but are alive, fluid, pulsing, seething, erupting, undulating, placid, or churning like the changing surface of the sea. Thus we are a part of a restless sea of meanings produced by persons, animate and inanimate nature, and organizations.

A second source of awareness is our receptivity to the stimulus inherent in these relationships. We ourselves choose whether to see, hear and feel this stimulus or not. Many of us are deaf, blind, and unfeeling. We have eyes that see not, ears that hear not, and a personal structure that protects us from the questions and messages that should be calling us out of our isolation. We pass a tree, but fail to see its color, texture, form, movement and sound, and we remain untouched by its gift of grace and beauty. We transact business, blindly unaware of the persons with whom we deal, and so remain unchallenged and unrenewed. We will go to a concert because such cultural endeavors need support, but the language of the symphonic enterprise, the team work of conductor and players, of instruments, of composer and producers, to say nothing of the music itself, may never reach us. Yet life should be a constant outpouring of stimuli, a richness of offering that defies description.

A third source of awareness is our active response to stimulus. For example, with music we should find and feel the rhythm of the music and respond to it internally or externally, depending on circumstances. At a concert we have to listen in an open but outwardly controlled way, but at home we can listen and respond with our whole bodies swinging, dancing, and giving free and spontaneous release to all that the music calls forth in us. Thus the body as well as the soul becomes a part of the music. It is important, when we are stimulated, to translate insight into action as soon as possible. The failure to build feeling into response will result in the loss of the power of feeling. Response aids the simultaneous assimilation of meaning and feeling, and thus creates and energizes new powers for further expression and action.

Awareness and the Expression of Feeling

It is important to experience grief and to express our experience of grief not only in words but with tears, and this holds true for men as well as for women. It is important to feel joy, and not only to tell somebody that we feel joyful, but to express the joy in actions appropriate to the feeling. If we feel love, and the urgency for its sexual expression, it is much better to express it in relationships which are appropriate, than it is to engage in conversations about love and sex or take courses in the subject or read books about it that can give only a superficial expression and release.

Many of us have feelings of guilt, are uneasy with our feelings, try to disguise them and express them in sneaky ways, thereby robbing ourselves of the clean flow of the fullness of our own natures. These unacknowledged feelings are often seduced by magazine and TV advertising so that we associate them with some product and its possession rather than acknowledging and expressing them. In such situations our feelings are manipulated by somebody else rather than expressed responsibly by us. In such situations we forfeit the satisfaction which comes from expressing and managing our own feelings.

Frequently the inability to express our feelings creatively is a result of the inhibitions of our middle-class conventions or of an overcerebralized education that emphasized the acquisition of knowledge and skills rather than sensitivity to the data of our senses and the power of human feelings. The exclusive emphasis on ideas, knowledge, and the skills that qualify a person to be a doer has molded us to respond only verbally to situations and to dissociate from them our true feelings. This kind of reaction has also been reinforced by the failure of religious teaching to cultivate an understanding of the whole man. Thus heavy emphasis has been placed on children being "good" with the implication, and sometimes with the direct teaching, that if they are not, they are not acceptable and God will not love them. Also adult worship has been too cerebral, ignoring feelings, especially negative ones. This neglect of the whole man on the part of religion and education has contributed in our day to the growing incidence of psychosomatic illness, the proneness to violence, and the need for drugs as an aid either to escape feeling or to induce an artificial "high."

There are many ways of taking a trip without having to resort to drugs. One is the development of our senses to both activate and receive communication. Since our education may not have trained us to use these resources for awareness, we ourselves must assume responsibility for their training. Many of us, for example, use our eyes exclusively. When we look at someone, we keep him "over there," distant from us—that is, we use our eyes in an alienating fashion and in support of our own alienation. We look at people warily rather than with awareness. Practice looking at people inclusively; bring them within the circle of your concern by the very way in which you look at them. Seek to include them totally with all their meanings and uncertainties. This is what is meant by having eyes that see. We can also train our other senses in awareness by the simple exercise of closing our eyes and forcing ourselves to use these other senses as the means of "seeing" the world. Try to "see" a flower with your fingertips and your sense of smell; try to see a tree with your hands, experiencing the texture of the bark, the shape and direction of the branches; try smelling the trunk and the leaves—even taste the bark and the leaves. Close your eyes and listen to the wind; feel it against your face and body.

In the practice of inclusion we use all avenues of awareness in order to open ourselves to the full potentiality of experience, to the total feeling and meaning conveyed. This is especially true in the case of feelings where openness is indispensable. We should never suppress our awareness of feeling, for feeling is an energy force that either fights or helps one. Our functioning as persons calls for the cooperation of all aspects of the self, including emotion and feeling. A person who is able to feel and to include what he feels in the meaning of an experience functions as a person with more profound awareness than one who is too restricted to feel what is really happening.

In time and with practice we can also acquire the ability to employ language in such a way that our words express the reality of which we are aware, including the feelings that permeate it. This honesty of language, uncomfortable as it may be to some at times, means being true to the situation in which we and the others find ourselves. To have feelings that are congruent with our understanding of a situation means being able to decide, speak, and act responsibly out of our feelings in relation to the feelings of others.

The Risks in Inclusive Awareness

The inclusionist, too, faces dangers. He runs the risk, because of his inclusionism, of becoming overstimulated on the one hand, or immune to stimulation on the other. In this culture, for instance, it is possible to become so overstimulated sexually that a person loses the ability to be aroused and to exercise his sexual powers. Or we can be so surfeited with sound that we become unresponsive to sound and develop an uncomprehending deafness. All of which means that an inclusionist needs a philosophy and discipline that will guide his practice of inclusion. Otherwise he can become a licentious consumer of sensation. A disciplined inclusionist is able both to accept and to reject, to be aroused or to remain passive, to speak or to remain silent, to listen or to turn off his listening, to view or not to view his television, or to turn it on only when he is responding to an interest that he wants to include as input for his education or pleasure. He is able to buy or not to buy, to accept invitations or to decline them, to go or to stay at home, to be a member of the crowd or to rejoice in solitariness;

to be, in other words, real and congruent in the decisions he makes about his participation in his total environment.

The following offer ways of avoiding the dangers of inclusion:

1. Accept the need for times of assimilation of new data and experiences. The purpose of inclusion is to increase the quality of life and not its quantity. Time for reflection after a peak experience will, then, enable us to sort out the meanings of the experience and build them into our value structure.

2. Beware of the evils of surfeiting. Too much of anything, no matter how excellent, may dull our capacity to appreciate. There are times when we need to turn off our awareness and rest in order that when we turn it on again, its power may be renewed.

3. Thoughtful choice from among the options for inclusion is important. Not every potential for inclusion can or should be included. I am not ready for some; others do not fit into my value system (although my value system needs a variety of stimuli to keep it growing).

4. A growing awareness of who I am and the choices appropriate for me is a basis for avoiding a sloppy kind of inclusion.

In order to make appropriate decisions, it is necessary for a person to have some kind of philosophy of life, some kind of faith in God and man, some standard of values and sense of integrity which will make it possible for him to be both independent of and dependent on what others think and feel.

Free to Be Aware

What kind of philosophy, religion, or standard of values must an individual have in order to be free to be himself in both thought and feeling? Put simply, this

person must be a caring person. He cares about both
others and himself; he cares about his environment and
about what happens to people. He cares about beauty
and is sensitive to its presence in what, on the surface,
may seem to be ugly. He cares about little things as well
as big. He cares about thoughtfulness. He cares enough
to disturb his own comfort. He cares about mankind and
its future. He cares about what he cannot see and what
he cannot understand because he knows it is important
to others. This kind of caring person is what we mean
when we say that an individual is a loving person. His
love, in the final analysis, is his willingness to be responsible for others, for himself, for the world in which he
lives, even if such responsibility is onerous and makes
upon him, what others would call, inordinate demands.

Such a caring person can be trusted, his feelings can be
trusted, and we can trust his expression of feeling. We
will find that his expression of feeling usually agrees with
his thoughts. Education and religion could be more effective in helping us to be more creatively real and congruent. The accumulation of knowledge and the acquisition of skills without reference to their relational
balance leaves the so-called educated man without capacity for realizing a high percentage of his potentiality.
On the other hand, ridiculous results occur when feelings
are divorced from intelligence, and sincerity and trans-
parency are recognized as the only virtues. Intense emotional immediacy, which is often encouraged by the
human potential movement, can lead nowhere because
the expression of feeling as an end in itself is not an adequate or dependable goal. A growing number of people
seem to be substituting the satisfactions and pains of encounter group experiences for the goal of becoming more
adequate in their permanent relationships. The leaders of
some training centers are beginning to restrict the en-

rollment of people who seem to have become addicted
to group experiences in place of responsible living. Unless
a person plans, decides, and acts responsibly, his spontaneous feelings degenerate into mere sentimentality
and erotic mischief. The temptation is great to substitute sensation for personal actualization. When we
succumb to that temptation, we become uncaring persons, who hinder the movement of the human race from
the biological level of being to the psychosocial or
spiritual level, which is essential if men are to have a
future.

In contrast, a caring person shines like a precious gem
in the fabric of mankind and, in the language of religion,
becomes for others a "means of grace." This phrase is
one usually used to designate the Bible, sacraments,
prayer, and the other sources through which Christians
believe they receive help from God. But the phrase has a
much broader reference than the specifically religious
one. Grace is favor, good will, compassion, caring. Fundamentally it is the action of one person in behalf of another; and religious people who understand in any depth
how God works realize that such actions are means by
which he conveys his grace. A grace-full person, then, is
one who is fully aware of himself as a person with power
to care and love, to forgive and heal. He is also aware
that it is possible for him to grow in such awareness, and
that other people are more than they appear to be. A
grace-full person is one who knows that there is the
demonic in him that can cause him to betray his power
to be a means of grace. A grace-full person is one who is
aware of his environments, physical and personal, and is
aware that he can abuse and destroy them. A grace-full
person is aware that man is in a period of transition and
that the decisions which we now make both individually
and corporately are crucial for the future. A grace-full

person is aware that without his responsible action, the presence of God in this society is to that extent diminished.

The thought that an individual can have this kind of power in relation to other persons staggers many and often shocks church people, who regard the idea as irreverent. I believe that the church is meant to be a fellowship of persons into whose care all means of grace are given. The problem is that church teaching tends to be so preoccupied with the subject matter of faith that it neglects the personal, incarnational part of its teaching. But without the awareness of this interpersonal means of grace underlying sacraments, rites, preaching, and institutional programs, the latter become life*less*, rather than life-*giving* forms. When we think of religion only in terms of theology, ritual, and morality, we become separated from its re-creative, redeeming source. The church, then, as a means of grace is basically the fellowship of persons who live for each other, are strong for those who are weak, and accept the strength of others in their own times of weakness; who believe for those who doubt, and because of the belief of others have the courage to accept and wrestle with their own doubt; who forgive the guilty with the forgiveness wherewith they were forgiven. In this context the traditional means of grace take on new meaning and power. We need also to remember that the only means of grace that most people in the world experience is the sacrament of the interpersonal, where the smile or the touch becomes the outward and visible sign of an inward and invisible reality of love, forgiveness, and healing.

The Inclusionist as Bearer of Grace

An inclusionist is both a giver and a receiver of grace, and thus continues to be a growing person. If he is in trouble and in need of help, he is able to include himself in relation to a helper, and if another is in need of help, he is able to include the other as one whom he can help, receiving him, listening to him, and responding to him out of his resources in such a way as to make available to him a new awareness of his own resources. The act of inclusion is always an act of courage. It takes courage to ask for help and to receive it, and to affirm oneself as needing help in a mature, noninfantile way. It also takes courage to give help, to affirm oneself as ready to help with no strings attached.

The inclusionist, accordingly, rejoices in the fact that a natural human relationship can heal and restore life, and in such a relationship he can be a representative and agent of the Creator and the Redeemer. One does not have to be ordained in order to be a pastor. This is a vocation open to all—secretary, milkman, insurance salesman, foreman, executive, lawyer, clerk, artist, or policeman—to any person whose awareness and sensitivity permit him to become an instrument of healing to those who are hurt, or of reconciliation to those who are alienated, and thus to affirm and restore them by giving them the courage for a new "go" at living.

Unfortunately the helping role too often tends to become institutionalized. When people ask for help, they get stones for bread. Young people, for instance, often raise questions that older people should responsibly listen to and consider. They should affirm the right of youth to question, because each new generation, for the sake of mankind's growth, must, in honesty, test what they are receiving from the past. But when youth do so, they are given moldy, irrelevant answers or insultingly told that when they are older they will know better. We may commend to them the rite of bread and wine, but without an enabling base and significance in the interpersonal and incarnational, the bread and wine are nothing more to them than bread and wine. Back of the bread and wine, it is essential that there stand the personal love, support, trust, and patience that must infuse every aspect and form of life, without which no question can be faced and no future contemplated.

Christians always face the temptation of using the teachings and practices of religion in a way to keep people at a safe distance, thus institutionalizing our responses. To hear and respond to another person or to a group of persons, especially those who are in distress or come with ontological questions, demands courage on our part to meet the courage of the person who is voicing the distress or asking the question. The latter needs to be met with encouragement, and we need to meet him with courage. At other times, according to circumstances, the need of each may be reversed so that the one who normally gives, receives; the one who receives, gives. Actually, in a relationship of grace, the benefits are mutual. The helper is helped by helping, and the helped helps by accepting help. Many times in my career as a pastor I have been called on for help at times when it seemed to me that I had nothing to give. But after having made an effort to respond, I discovered that I was engaging in a mutual process of help and renewal.

What is required of us if we would be the means of grace to another? The first requirement is that we listen. There is nothing startling about this response, but it is an indispensable and fundamental one. The capacity for listening is rare among us. Many of us listen out of our respective agenda anxieties and our preoccupations. We preclude real listening because of the image of the person we have in mind so that the meaning of what he is saying is distorted by this image. We also lower our level of listening by our preoccupation with what we want to say, and by our search for an opening in which to make our speech. And sometimes we listen fearful of what we may hear, because if we really heard what the other person was saying, we would be confronted, judged, and called forth by him into making possible changes.

Listening is an act of love, an act of caring, a commitment of ourselves to another. We should listen with every sense—that is, sensitively—if we are responsibly and reverently to participate in the mystery of another human being. Listening is not a one-sided activity. The other person calls to us in all kinds of ways. He wants to be heard, because to be heard is to be known, and to be known is to live. Listening should always be two-sided: the speaker respects the listener by trying to speak his meanings clearly and honestly, and the listener respects the speaker by giving his whole attention to what the speaker is trying to say.

What does listening accomplish? Not only does it give us indispensable information, but it is the act which enables us to participate in the union of man with man. Listening bridges the separation between man and man, and may be the means by which our reunion with God and man is initiated.

What do we listen for? Do we listen to detect the failures of others, to sit in judgment of their confusions and inadequacies? Do we listen in order to rejoice in our superiority? Do we listen in order to make sure that they are safely separated from us by misunderstandings that will permanently keep us apart? Or, on the other hand, do we listen to discover the signs of their achievement, power, and integrity? Do we listen for testimony of their growth and awareness and for indications of their readiness to include us? These are the questions to ask ourselves about the adequacy and quality of our listening.

Again, with what feelings do we listen? with our envy

and jealousy? with our fear? Do we listen with our resentment? Do we listen with the smallness of our uncorrected image of them? Do we listen with our prejudice? Do we just pretend to listen, while we pursue our own preoccupations? Do we listen with our feelings of despair, despondency, and cynicism?

Or do we listen with compassion, understanding, and trust? Do we listen, having in mind the allowances which must be made for the frailty of human beings, for the contradictions in all of us? Do we listen with the expectation that our understanding of the person will grow? Do we remember the depressing effect of having been listened to by a person who had low expectations of us? In our very listening we have the power to increase or diminish the lives and meanings of the people associated with us. An inclusionist never forgets this tremendous power which he possesses.

Second, if I would be an instrument of grace to others, it is required that I participate with them in a true meeting which begins, as we have seen, with the act of speaking and listening. Participation means becoming another's partner in the enterprise of healing or, to state it more generally, in the enterprise of becoming, which is the main business of living. In a business enterprise a partner is a person who invests himself and his money in the enterprise; his resources are committed to it. So too the inclusionist, the caring person, has a tremendous awareness of what it means to be a partner as a parent, friend, therapist, or fellow pilgrim through the complicated and sometimes tortuous passages of life. As partner, he commits what he is as a person—his life, his being, his values, his beliefs, his knowledge, his skills; and in so doing he takes tremendous risks—the risk of creativity, the risk of loving, the risk of trusting, and finally the risk of having his gift rejected. It is truly appalling to realize

how many people simply want to play it safe and exclude
the possibility of risk, or be assured of substantial reward
if they are to make the gift of themselves; and when
they are not assured of reward, they refuse to make the
gift. These people diminish and destroy life. It would be
bad enough if their defensiveness destroyed only their
own life, but the tragedy is that their stinginess, based on
fear, is destructive of the increase of life upon which the
very future of man depends.

The inclusionist gives himself in order to affirm the
other, and in his affirmation of others, he affirms himself.
This kind of affirmation, of course, does not mean un-
qualified approval of what some person does and what
other people think and do. A teenager was caught with
possession of a large amount of marijuana which he expected to sell. A friend was with him at the time and
had no knowledge of the drug. The young man with the
drug testified to his friend's innocence. The judge knew
both boys, and because of his belief in their basic char-
acters, dismissed the case against the second boy, and
postponed action on the first for a year pending demonstrations of good behavior. Both experienced affirmation
from the judge. The experience of being affirmed and
accepted must include the experience of being judged,
and this holds true both for the inclusionist and for the
person included. For the inclusionist, whatever happens
is curriculum. He is able to use whatever occurs as a
result of his communication with others as a source of
learning and as a base for further participation which,
one hopes, will eventually produce insight and growth.
In this matter, the exclusionist is judgmental and condemns, whereas the inclusionist gives the judgments of
love and affirmation which, while they can be stern and
overwhelming, are nevertheless enabling because the
judged continues to be held in respect as a person.

The inclusionist also understands the role that guilt plays in communication, whereas the exclusionist is likely to be searching for self-justification regardless of guilt. We all have our areas of guilt and our guilt feelings. When we seek to participate in life, this guilt needs to be acknowledged. It is not adequately acknowledged when acceptance is interpreted as approval. The reality of our guilt and our feelings of guilt can only be dealt with when acknowledged seriously and, in spite of our guilt, we are accepted. And it is only when we consciously accept this acceptance, that we are restored in the relationship and able to participate in it fully. This is the pattern of true repentance.

The inclusionist also has to be aware of the need for dialogue.* Listening and participation produce the agenda of relationship that must be dealt with if growth is to follow. The unwillingness to deal with this agenda (disagreements, problems, etc.) is one of the primary reasons why most people are unable to grow and why their relationships deteriorate. In order to keep a spurious peace, people turn aside from the issues of disagreement that may be developing; such is, of course, no peace at all, and our life turns out to be lacking in growth. The inclusionist is willing to include the pain which a relationship entails for the sake of the achievements possible in the relationship. He is aware that there can be no growth without pain. He knows that without the acceptance of pain as a part of life, his only alternative is the pain of death: the death of possibilities, the death of relationships, and the death of all meaning, which will make old age a time of misery and his ultimate physical death an ignoble end.

As I said earlier, we narrowly restrict our idea of a

---

* See Reuel L. Howe, *The Miracle of Dialogue* (New York: The Seabury Press, 1963).

means of grace to the church's religious rites, and we avoid facing the fact that most of the people will never enter a church or encounter the means of grace usually found there. The only means of grace available to these people will be that which comes from and through the persons with whom they have some association, and who, through word or action, convey to them the gifts of God's love and acceptance. Any responsible, concerned person may be a means of God's grace. And if there is to be a creative response to our contemporary problems, it will be as men accept their roles as agents of the gifts of love, caring, and healing, and making their lives sacraments of the personal.

Communicating Awareness

Inclusionists are also aware that communication, in addition to its verbal aspects, includes nonverbal means of conveying a message. Man has communicated non-verbally much longer than he has by words, and he still uses this primordial means despite his acquired verbal skills. The basic emotions, which are instinctual and primitive, manifest themselves usually in and through bodily expressions. We pretend to be more rational and verbal than we really are, and are therefore often unaware of contrary meanings we unconsciously express through nonverbal means. In fact, a person expresses only about thirty-five or forty percent of his meanings verbally. The remainder he expresses through the action of his body. I have watched with amazement a therapist help people with their emotional problems simply by observing them and working with their bodily tensions. His insights were unbelievably accurate and always on target in relation to their need and condition. I asked him how this could be. His answer was simple. "Men lie with their lips, but not with their bodies." What he meant was that with our words we can misrepresent our feelings and our concerns, but those who can read the language of the body are not deceived by such misrepresentation; to them the body reveals a person's true condition. We all need to be more aware of body language and the large part of our communication it expresses.

How do we develop our awareness of body language? How do we begin to understand its message? We begin by broadening our "listening" to include the signals of body behavior and studying its meaning in ourselves and others. We can ask ourselves about our own body responses, and discuss with others the meaning of their body behavior, listening carefully to their verbal attempts to interpret it. And here it is imperative that we resist making snap judgments about body language, for it can be easily misinterpreted. The same behavior (laughing, crying, silence, jumpiness) can signify various meanings and be variously interpreted. Crying, for instance, may signify either joy or sadness, and many is the poor husband who has been confused over the meaning of his wife's weeping. Drooping shoulders may represent discouragement, despair, or weariness. If we are not careful, the interpretation we give to an action may be false for the person we are observing but true in relation to our own inner condition and expectations of him. Such misinterpretations do much harm to human relations. Our nonverbal language should reinforce our verbal.

The question, then, whether the language of our words correlates with the language of our bodies is an important and serious one. For when they do not correlate, our communication is confused, and the problems of living together are further complicated. We need to realize that the ear is the organ for receiving the verbal communication, and the eye for receiving the nonverbal or body language. Listening, then, is done with both the eye and the ear. The function of the eye and the ear, to use a computer term, is to "program" our communications, to furnish the data to which our responses are to make reply.

As communicators, we need feedback in order that we may know how others see and "read" us and how we see and "read" them. By this feedback we can begin to learn to correlate our verbal and nonverbal language so that people will not receive from us contradictory messages. The same feedback will save us from naïve interpretations of others' communications. While it is true that men's words are supposed to represent them truly, their words, because of the depth of meaning out of which they speak, may not represent all that they are attempting to say.

Inclusionists sometimes have to employ the nonverbal as a substitute for verbal language. On one occasion I had to teach a group whose language I neither spoke nor understood. In the course of these sessions I was interested to discover how much I was able to learn about their responses from facial expressions, tones of voice, and bodily actions, before their verbal responses were actually translated. I was impressed with the universality of nonverbal language. Regardless of our different verbal languages, body language seems to convey the same meaning everywhere. The same gestures and expressions were used for puzzlement, pleasure, amusement, amazement, anger, and love. One wonders what kind of world could be created if men learned to depend more on nonverbal communication than on their more complicated and not so dependable verbal language.

Inclusionists also are aware that some meanings are beyond the power of our words to express. Rapture cannot be adequately verbalized, nor can love. The lover requires the eloquence of action which conveys meanings that words alone cannot express, but the message of love's action needs the assistance of the words of love because the words help to identify the meaning of the act. Furthermore, while body language may be less controlled consciously, yet it cannot be completely trusted, and so for another reason verbal assistance is sometimes needed to guide its interpretation. We may see expressions of pain, for example, and not know the reasons for the pain.

This interdependence between verbal and nonverbal is seen in our larger corporate relationships. We often verbalize the need of justice and equality for all men. The words alone, however, have never been able to accomplish needed change in race relations, for example, until action became the bearer of the meaning. It was only then that witness became effective, because action introduced the missing element of relationship. Men and women met (from all parts of the country in one place), acted (demonstrations, marches, prayers, sacraments) regardless of denominational affiliations and differences, and suffered (beatings, deaths, imprisonments, loss of jobs, ridicule, misinterpretation). The message of these nonverbal actions provided substantiating and illustrative meanings to their words. The teaming up of word and action would go a long way toward bringing us nearer to the solution of many crucial problems in this time of transition.

5. Discerning Time and Its Rhythms

Many of us think of the journey through life from birth to death as being made on a paved highway called "Time," which stretches ahead endlessly although our journey paces only a short span of it. This highway was there before we arrived and will wind its way on after we leave it. Our march, however, seems often to be a forced one through crises and transitions so that we are frustrated by and resent the pace at which we are driven forward. A strong sense of finiteness and incompleteness is always with us.

We did not always experience time in this way. In childhood time seemed endless. Then, the time between birthdays or Christmases was an eternity. In youth we spent much energy wishing time away. I can remember wishing that I were twelve, eighteen, or twenty-one, and it seemed as if such momentous moments would never come. Such was our awareness of being that all experience seemed timeless.

Clock and Calendar Time

There are, then, two ways of thinking about time, two kinds of time. There is clock (and calendar) time, and there is time for being. The former, clock time, is tyrannical, a relentless master driving and pressuring us onward without regard or concern of any kind. Of course, it is not really the clock which does this to us; it is our own learned response to the clock. By rigid adherence to clock time we mechanize our lives and ultimately depersonalize ourselves. And while we have our moments of rebellion, we usually feel guilty about being inactive, "goofing off," "wasting time." This has been a legacy of Puritan ethos which declared work to be the only justified use of time. Some people today are attempting to escape this servitude to clock time, but unfortunately they rush to the opposite extreme and cast away all respect for time; by doing so, they eventually repudiate responsibility for themselves and others. But most people respond to the tyranny of clock time by immersing themselves in their routines or settling into ruts to avoid facing the stresses of being and thinking about their lives and actions. People fall into all kinds of ruts: the rut of making love in the same way; the rut of driving the same route from work to home; the rut of thinking the same thoughts and having the same reactions to similar experiences; the rut of voting a party ticket without evaluation of candidates and issues; of continuing traditional beliefs and practices with a closed mind; the rut of looking at the same type of television programs. Any and every rut is a threat to being and an obstacle to growth; and every life lived in ruts by its very inertia drags mankind back to some lower level of existence and being. The old evangelical hymn, "Take Time to Be Holy," had a point. We might rephrase it by saying, "Take time to be."

There can be no question that clock time is indispensable for living. We must become aware, however, of its limitations and the need for another kind of time in our lives if we are to achieve growth and survival. Let us see what happens when clock time is our sole master.

First, clock time restricts our vision, and we are aware only of the narrow task at hand to be completed. As I write this, I am overwhelmed by the sense of my own self and what is happening in what I call myself. It is full of wonder: my heart is beating; my lungs are breathing rhythmically; my blood is coursing through my veins; my digestive organs are functioning; my muscles are at work transforming through some mysterious process my thoughts and feelings into printed symbols which can be read by others and transformed back into thoughts and feelings that can affect their heartbeat, breathing, circulation, and capacity for relationship. Such an enriching moment of awareness and contemplation as this almost never occurs when, clock-bound, we push ahead with our limited, assigned task. Moreover, such awareness is part of the religious process of being aware, the way of contemplating the glory, beauty, mystery, and wonder of God and the world he created. But to experience such awareness we must be free to break loose from the pressures of chronological time.

Second, rigid obedience to clock time prevents us from responding to what is appropriate to the occasion. The clock tells us that it is time to leave, and therefore we must engage in behavior that is appropriate to leaving despite what may be developing of a relational nature. The relationship, for example, may be so delicately balanced that the interruption tips matters to the side of alienation. Often the clock pushes us into actions for which we are inadequately prepared; we act without reflection, assimilation, and formulation, the necessary preparations for action. This tyranny of chronological time plays havoc with education. Because there is only so much time in which to fill the "void" in the student's mind with information, the teacher's agenda-anxiety cannot pause to respond respectfully to the integrity of the student and his pace of learning.

Third, we lose poise when we make the clock our god. There is something frantic about the way people live and move when a sense of being is absent. Their movements, whether physical, psychological, or spiritual, have a breathlessness and jumpiness about them that makes the whole world seem jerky and frenzied. It is interesting that at the very period when this condition has become so prevalent in society, there should be a turning on the part of sizable numbers toward religions of contemplation and meditation, in which quietness, poise, and serenity are so prominent. Many people are now finding time to be religious, although many adherents of the standard religions are too busy racing the clock to explore the depths of the faith they profess in terms of a quality of life.

Fourth, slavery to clock and calendar has deprived us of time to cultivate wisdom. Knowledge we have, also technology. Healthy relationships we have not, because we are without wisdom. Wisdom is the ability to discern inner qualities and essential relationships, an ability which requires time to simmer and distill the essential meaning of experience. George and Betts had only twelve hours together before he had to go overseas. At first they were frantic because of the shortness of time available to them and its rapid passing. At last they decided to ignore clock time and respond to life time. Their wise decision made their time together more precious and lasting. They not only kept alive in the face of threatening circumstances, but actually achieved increase of life. This insight has meaning for what we might call "throw-away-marriages," namely, short-time attempts at finding fulfillment. People who look for instant relationships are afraid to use time for the exploration of personal and relational being.

There are occasions, of course, when it is important for us to be prompt, regardless of life time. Inclusionists hold promptness in tension with other values. The machine is geared to clock time, not to being-time, and we do have to make adjustments to the machine's influence on life. As inclusionists we must participate in a dialogue with the machines that serve us in order to avoid becoming intimidated by the machine and functioning like automatons. The machine can be either a friend or an enemy. The automobile, for example, as it is now used in response to the pressures of clock time is in many ways an enemy to man. Unless we are able to develop a new relationship between the machine and man, technology of itself will not save or improve the quality of time.

Yes, it is necessary in this life to be able to "tell" time, but the question is: What kind of time are we able to tell? Are we focused on clock time, or on life time which manifests itself in rhythms, seasons, occasions of joy and celebration, tragedies, movements, growth, and anything else that makes for the fullness of time? To experience fullness of time means recovering our total capacity for relationship with ourselves, others, and nature—for we depend upon all of them. Many people have lost—and many more are going to lose—this sense of fullness of time. In my neighborhood, many new houses are being built. So impatient are their owners that they produce instant gardens. One day the ground is bare; the next day there is a green lawn with full-grown bushes and trees and flowers that literally have appeared overnight. Today we are too impatient to plant a seed and wait for it to grow and produce. Our association with the machine has caused us to lose the sense of joy in gestation and production. We want not only instant gardens, but instant relations, instant joy, instant achievement, instant life of every kind.

The foregoing discussion should not be interpreted as meaning that we have to make an absolute choice between the fullness of time and chronological time. What is being suggested is that we need to make them inclusive of each other. Inclusionists value the quality of time and include and subordinate its quantitative measurement. Thus they are able to achieve a sense of timing that helps them to become more aware, to grow, to escape mechanized death. Exclusionists, on the other hand, reject the quality of time—that is, time for being—in favor of quantitative time, their focus being on "spending" or "filling" it, regardless of meaning.

Life and Time for Being

Life is a series of physiological, psychological, and economic rhythms. Our biological functions, for example, are on-and-off systems, including the heartbeat, respiration, elimination, and reproduction. We know, for example, that human beings can make love at almost any time, but there are times when it is better than others. We are more capable of dealing with difficulties at one time than another. Even some diseases have an on-and-off rhythm. There is a liver tumor, for instance, that is on a known twenty-four-hour cycle which begins at a specific time, say, 8:00 A.M. This tumor is extremely resistant to anticancer drugs, unless the drug is given just before 8:00 A.M. Then it is extremely susceptible to the drug, because it seems to be attacking the rhythm system.

Men have known about the rhythms of human relationship for centuries. Ecclesiastes describes them beautifully:

> For everything there is a season, and a time for every matter under heaven:
>
> a time to be born, and a time to die;
> a time to plant, and a time to pluck up what is planted;
> a time to kill, and a time to heal;
> a time to break down, and a time to build up;
> a time to weep, and a time to laugh;
> a time to mourn, and a time to dance;
> a time to cast away stones, and a time to gather stones together;
> a time to embrace, and a time to refrain from embracing;
> a time to seek, and a time to lose;
> a time to keep, and a time to cast away;
> a time to rend, and a time to sew;
> a time to keep silence, and a time to speak;
> a time to love, and a time to hate;
> a time for war, and a time for peace.

And we might add:

> A time for intimacy and a time for distance;
> a time for advance and a time for withdrawal;
> a time for passion and a time for quiescence.

These rhythms are resources for our living. Inclusionists accept and use them. It is important, then, to be aware of our own time patterns and those of others, and to assist one another in recognizing them. If we do not know, we should ask; if our partner, whether in marriage, business, or profession, seems ignorant or unheeding, we should include ourselves by letting him or her know what our rhythm needs are, while at the same time trying to be aware of his or her rhythm needs. Members of an organization who realized that a colleague was going through a marital crisis reduced the pressure on him by assuming more responsibility. In his anxious and disturbed state of being, they functioned protectively.

Our understanding and use of time will improve as we grow and acquire new values for the next stage of our development. No longer is it enough to be a college graduate, because the same instant that one graduates, what he was and knew becomes obsolete in relation to the changes that already have begun in him and are occurring in the world in which he lives. We are fond of saying that "time marches on." Perhaps it does. The real question is, do we march on? We have another saying: "Time heals all wounds." Is it time that heals, or is it what happens in the passing of time that heals? These are illustrations, again, of how important being is in relation to time. Then too, we often think of history as happenings within the stream of time. It is unfortunate that many of us have learned history mostly in terms of dates and the measurement of linear time, rather than learning from it the lessons of men's interactions with each other.

The Interrelation of Past and Present

We are all products of times past; we participate at least nominally in times present; and we are headed toward, and should be preparing for, times future. Implicit in everything we do are the meanings of time past, time present, and time future. When I cast my vote, which is a present-day action, I do so in the context of a history that has produced the present system and condition of government and contributed to the issues and personalities in relation to which I cast my vote. But my vote is a here-and-now event in which I not only participate but am, if I am a conscientious citizen, completely involved. In casting my vote, I have to make decisions about the here and now that are my own decisions. I cannot vote Republican because my father was a Republican. What he was influences me, but I have to become who I am in order to do what I have to do now. Thus there is both continuity and discontinuity between the past and the present. Unfortunately, however, too many people are prisoners of the past when they perform present acts.

My present act, however, has meaning for the future, because it contributes to the conditions which will prevail tomorrow. And so there is an intimate relationship between yesterday, today, and tomorrow. Neither one can be understood by itself. Neither one should have dominance over the other two, and the relationship between them must be inclusive.

Exclusionists, however, tend to break up the intimacy between yesterday, today, and tomorrow. Some exclusionists find the sole focus of meaning in the past. They are traditionalists whose anthem is, "As it was in the beginning, is now, and ever shall be." They want things to remain the way they are. Exclusionists are always hounded by the domination of memory and are never free of the past. Their gods are always the gods of the dogmas of the past. Their manners are determined by the conventions of the past. Their fears are rooted in past experiences. Their hopes are blasted because the past is no more. The traditionalist's political, social, and religious beliefs are rarely relevant because he excludes and separates them from the present. The present, for a traditionalist, is a time for the reincarnation of the past, and the future is a hypothetical occasion in which he expects his present views based on the past to be vindicated.

This does not mean that tradition does not have a place and that history does not provide significant rootage for finding the meanings of the present. The comments at this point have to do with the exclusionist traditionalist, whom I earlier referred to as people who walk backward into history, looking fondly in the direction of the founding fathers and apostles.

There is also another type of exclusionist, the activist exclusionist. His interest is only in the present. He excludes the past and the lessons that it offers and has, therefore, no context for contemporary decision. He is an isolationist in the sense that he does not want to join his work to that of men who have gone before. He sees only discontinuity and thinks that in dealing with present problems it is necessary to start from scratch. He excludes the best of tradition, but he is also cavalier about the future, and is therefore doubly irresponsible.

The opposite form of exclusionism is to be found in the dreamer. His visions are of the good things to come. He is impatient with the present problems and crises and has a tendency to idolize the future; thus he excludes from the past and the present the real lessons that at least partly precondition the future. He substitutes fantasies and theorizing about possibilities in place of instructive remembrance of things past and responsible action for the present. These kinds of exclusionists are to be found among the communes and other utopian endeavors.

What is needed instead is an inclusive relation between yesterday, today, and tomorrow. The door of communication is through the present, where we can

turn left into the long and complicated corridors of
history, or turn right into the open spaces of the un-
formed possibilities of the future. Inclusionists hopefully
enter this door of the present with a sense of identity and
responsibility that will protect them from being dominated by the points of view and values of the past, while
at the same time they distill its lessons, cherish its continuity with the present, assimilate its wisdom, and build
on what men have done before. Because of this inherit-
ance, inclusionists are able to look squarely at the present, to see its problems and challenges, but also its
resources and possibilities. They accept contemporary
questions as being legitimate questions. They do not
allow these questions to make them defensive about what
they value in the past. Inclusionists accept the possibility that some forms of the past must die or be transformed or reformed, and they believe that love and
justice and human value will find appropriate forms in
each generation. Inclusionists give thought to history,
but they do not allow it to intimidate them. For they
accept the here and now as the arena for assimilating
the past and planning for the future, as well as for present
living. They maintain a dialogue between the meanings
that come out of their contemporary life and the meanings that came from history and tradition.

The inclusionist knows that the adequacy with which
he meets contemporary questions is dependent upon the
degree to which the dialogue between past and present
meanings is carried out honestly and courageously. If he
fails in this dialogue, he realizes that he has to meet the
persons and issues of his own time with two sets of
meanings—a situation confusing for him and for others.
For example, many church people live their church life
rooted only in the tradition out of which they come, and
they do not want this tradition to change. It is not

enough to venerate the Bible; its meaning must be tested by, and also deal with, the issues and challenges of the present. In economics the tradition of free enterprise must be in dialogue with the complexities and pressures of our present economic condition. In education the Mark Hopkins tradition of teacher and student on either end of a log must cope with the contemporary knowledge explosion and technological capability, to say nothing of our need for education that prepares men to live together. Traditionalists have contemporary responsibilities, and activists should remember that they live in a world that did not begin today.

Thus we see that the dialogue between the meanings of past and present produces the meanings with which we live and encounter others. This kind of inclusion between one's own and our culture's past and present prepares us to be more open to what happens.

Building a Known Future

So much for the dialogue between past and present. What about its relation to future time? We learn from the past, we act in the present, and we anticipate some kind of future. What that future will be we have no way of knowing. Neither can we apply to present situations lessons from the past and build a *known* future. We can only "risk" a future out of what we are, have, and can do. Our present actions and plans, profiting though they may from past lessons, can have only unforeseen consequences. With all our knowledge and technology and even with some relational capacity, we cannot design our future. We cannot know what the rest of the 1970s will bring and even less about succeeding decades. There are too many variables in our situation of which we are unaware and cannot predict. These variables exist in individuals, in our group life, and in our social and cosmic limitations and potentialities. Further, past, present, and future are not sequential and logical. Time is more than linear. Its meanings cannot be discerned by measurement. All the qualities of being are involved, interrelated and influential. We are faced with infinite complexity. In our future, which now we cannot discern, lie possibilities both exciting and creative, and horrendous and demonic.

The only preparation that we can make is an inclusionist one. We can studiously seek an awareness of the consequences of our present actions, realizing that our awareness will always be partial, but conceivably growing. We may seek to know and understand the story of our origins and history both as individuals and as a people living on this globe. The more clearly we can tell our story, the stronger a sense of identity grows. The most powerful stories are stories about being delivered from captivity: the Jews from captivity in Egypt, which led to their concept of being the "chosen people"; the blacks from centuries of slavery and discrimination, which emerges in their concept of "Soul" and that "Black is beautiful." With such identities men can move with courage, overcoming fear, into the doorways of present situations and into unknown futures. With a sense of identity we can risk the future, but not without pain, rebellion, self-examination, purging, and pursuit of a purpose.

What about us individually and culturally? Do we have a sense of identity that has the courage to risk the future? If not, what is the captivity from which we need deliverance that will open up the possibilities of the future for us? We are captives of illusions about ourselves as white though racist, adequate though ineffectual, powerful though misguided, right and righteous though wallowing in the mud of moral confusion and irresolution; deliverers of the world and yet in desperate need of being delivered from ourselves and our illusions about ourselves.

In such conditions the need for inclusion becomes apparent. An inclusionist is open to the possibility of surrendering his illusions about himself, accepting his need of help, and accepting the help that is always available among and through people. The inclusionist who accepts his need for help has already laid the foundation for a more secure and viable sense of identity. As a people we have a story to tell full of achievement and failure. But what is the present state of our story? Can we tell the present story of our confusion, self-doubt, fear, and arrogance with a sense that for the moment this *is* our part of the ongoing story? Can we be released from the captivity of our illusions and realize that others after us will begin to tell this as a part of their story? If so, then our sense of identity will return. With its return will come a freedom to maintain open attitudes toward change, conflict, and ambiguity, to provide relationships of dialogue which will strengthen and illumine us for coping with unforeseen variables.

With what concreteness can we approach this awesome task? The inclusionist way of living is a way of living simultaneously in open relation to the past, present, and future. This will require three actions on our part whether we are functioning as individuals or in our various kinds of human groupings: we must listen, speak, and then be prepared to deal with the results of listening and speaking.

Listening. Out of the meanings that come from the dialogue of our past and present, we will strive to *listen* inclusively to the meanings of others. With our own knowledge, insights, values, and convictions, we really *listen* with the hope of *hearing*. We want to hear the other for their sake, and with the expectation of learning from them; of increasing our own knowledge; of deepening our own values; and of broadening and strengthening our own convictions.

We will not necessarily accept and assimilate everything we hear. Some things we will reject and exclude, but not as exclusionists do. We exclude only after honest consideration of possibilities. Inclusionists use discretion in both their exclusioning and their inclusioning.

Speaking. Out of our meanings, we then *speak* inclusively to the meanings of others. Having heard them, we now *speak* responsively to them. That is, we maintain a tension between what we think and believe and feel, and the convictions and attitudes of others. Others in their turn, we hope, will *listen* inclusively, out of their meanings produced by their dialogue with their own past and present, to our meanings; and will also speak inclusively in response to what they hear.

Listening and Speaking. Such inclusive listening and speaking does not mean that the participants have to agree with each other. Agreement is not the first goal of communication. There may be rivalry and competition in communication, but the spirit and action of inclusion makes it creative. In a tennis match each player studies his opponent, his strengths and weaknesses, his style and rhythms, and plays inclusively in relation to the other, with the result that each plays a better game than he would otherwise. Some readers may question the tennis game analogy because they resent the suggestion that life is a game and that it is played to win. Life is in part a game, and it is lived to win, but win what? The time has come for us to play responsively to win a desire for cooperation, for community, for actualization and for individual and corporate futures.

Dealing with Results of Listening and Speaking. As a result of mutual inclusive speaking and listening, new content and new relationship is produced. Some of this is immediately productive and creative; some of it, however, presents problems of misunderstanding, resentment, and alienation. It becomes necessary, therefore, for the participants, having listened and spoken, to *deal* now with the new and troublesome communication situation that they have produced. At this point much human communication breaks down because people do not work at, or are afraid to *deal* with, the real issues in their relationships. They do not want to face the dangers and pains of doing so. Instead, they strive to maintain the thin and fragile covering of "peace at any price," with the result that they lose touch with each other, live in separated loneliness, and communicate only about the trivia of their relationship. In this state of being there is no meeting of real meaning between them.

On the other hand, people who will risk honest communication with each other about the real issues of their relationship may grow in love and mutual respect in spite of the pain and scars of communication. They may achieve relationships of depth and trust, and their future will continue to have promise.

Inclusion, therefore, requires that people *listen, speak,* and *deal.* These are the LSDs of communication and relationship and may be the means of a lively "trip" through life.

Out of the meeting of meaning that is produced by the practice of inclusion, the character and content of a dialogical relationship which should be useful in future dialogue begins to appear. Thus through the doorway of inclusion, as we have noted, we move onto the threshold of our future, open to the interactions of our meetings with one another, fed by our agonies and doubts, and by our risks and achievements.

So, in summary, out of the dialogue of the meanings of our tradition (past) and contemporary life (present), we meet each other inclusively and move into the new age (future) of our lives. Keeping alive means living out of our past, in relation to our present and toward our future. The future happens! We plan, discuss, and contribute intelligently or foolishly. The plan may not work, but because we planned and strove together responsibly in time present, something will materialize willy-nilly in the future which paradoxically will then be time present. The baton of meaning moves continuously and discontinuously through the generations toward either actualization or self-destruction. And so does mankind move slowly, irregularly, with retreat as well as advance, out of the past, through the present, into the future, experiencing, interpreting, acting, both inheriting and writing its story, which is both continuous and discontinuous.

Our discussion of time reveals a need. Life is lived in time, but time without meaning is empty and boring. But even the meaning must have certain characteristics if men are to grow beyond what they are. Left to themselves under the pressures of clock time they "mark time," live on already accrued but unrenewed interest, with only partially explored here-and-now perspectives. Growth and actualization require that we have times of celebration, festivity, and imaginative projection of ourselves into future possibilities in order to experience a fresh sense of purpose, love, and power to be. We need to recover old times and find new ones for celebration. Men need to dance, both literally and figuratively; and to dream beyond the reaches of their clutching realities. Gaity, joy, spontaneity, exuberance, playful love, and living play along with the more sober virtues of patience, kindness, and trust have the power to turn time into eternity. Remember, the twelve hours shared by George and Betts, because they celebrated their love, seemed timeless and full and running over.

6. Mastering Negative Experiences

Life cannot be lived without some negative experiences of fear, hatred, disagreements, impersonal treatment, or the like. Many people, if not most, have difficulty accepting these experiences as a part of their lives. They respond with a feeling of having been betrayed. But every negative belongs to a positive, and growth is accomplished by assimilating and integrating negative as well as positive experiences. If a person will not include the negative in his concerns, he cannot grow in his relationships. Hence a basic corollary of the principle of inclusion is: *the positive includes but subordinates the negative.*

The negative aspects of a relationship between a husband and wife, for example, have to be included in and subordinated to the positive power of their love. Unfaithfulness on the part of either of them has been regarded as a negative force working against their love.

This negative behavior does have meaning, but the important question is what the couple is going to do about it. Will they allow the meaning of the negative to destroy the positive power of their love and to alienate them further? Or can they accept the negative experience and allow it to become a source of learning and growth? For it is possible to turn an experience of mistrust into one that will, in the end, strengthen trust.

The practice of inclusion requires that we face up to and deal with all experiences that threaten us with the loss of love and life. Because these experiences are negative, we try to deny them. We resist anything that threatens loss of identity, prestige, power, love, money, or reputation, or that produces such basic reactions as fear, hatred, alienation, and death. If we are very defensive, we will be so threatened by the loss of anything that we have, that we will make futile and pathetic attempts to hold on to the little bit we have left. Exclusionists are so aware of what they might lose or have already lost that they fail to take into account what they still have. Inclusionists, on the other hand, take into account and accept what they have instead of concentrating their outlook on what they do not have. The result of such patterns is that exclusionists lose even what they have, while inclusionists are prepared to build on what they have, unhampered by considerations of what they lack.

The Origin of Certain Tensions

Let us go back to the beginnings of our personal lives for an explanation of this tension between the negative and the positive. We begin life with a need for mother and her care. We are so constituted that if this need is satisfied, all will be well for us, provided of course that our mother wants and loves us. The baby cannot feed himself; he is fed. He cannot guard and protect himself;

he is protected. All that the mother does to meet his various needs becomes a manifestation of her love. Her ministrations, including deprivations that she might have to make, are done in response to the baby's various needs, whether deficiency or growth needs. The different manifestations of her love give it reality and form. The child usually experiences feeding and bathing as pleasurable manifestations; being put down for a nap when he does not want it may seem to him not love, but rejection— the desire to be rid of him, as indeed in part it may be. But on the whole, if the situation is a reasonably healthy one, the child experiences the mother's love as positive.

But the mother also has fears and anxiety about her child's welfare. She is concerned that she might not be an adequate mother and, therefore, fail him; that no matter how loving and caring she might try to be, he still might suffer permanent and crippling deprivation. She is concerned that he might be alienated by her resentment of him at those times when she is feeling tired and inconvenienced by his care. *Her anxiety in his and her own behalf is the negative aspect of her love,* included in and subordinated to her positive expressions of love. *Both are necessary for the full love of another.* The fear and anxiety of a mother—the negative aspect of her love—is essential in motivating her thought and foresight in caring for her child. Without the negative force of anxiety, her love would be deficient and incomplete. Fear, then, when included in and subordinated to love, helps to make her love for her child strong and practical.

The same dynamic holds true for all other relationships. The love of a woman for what a man is must include and subordinate her anxiety about how she might fail him and how he might fail her; and similarly, the man's love for a woman must include his anxiety about his possible failure of her and about her disappointment in him. When the negative aspects of a relationship are included and subordinated to the positive, there is more possibility for growth in the relationship than when the negative and the positive are kept separate and experienced as unrelated. The negative by itself, then, has the power to alienate, and the positive does not have the possibility of asserting itself and growing because it does not have real work to do.

Returning again to the mother-child illustration, we should note that there are positive and negative aspects to the child's responses, which also include elements of love and fear. The cry for help is, for example, implicitly a fear of isolation and the possible loss of the mother, which would mean death. The child experiences the mother's presence as care and love. When he sees her leave him, the question arises in his mind, "Will she come back?" The longer he has to wait for her return, the more fearful and anxious he becomes, until he is overwhelmed by a sense of panic as to what will happen to him if she does not return. This is fear for one's self, which implicitly and ultimately is a fear of death. On the other hand, the sense of comfort accompanied by expressions of pleasure and being loved and cared for is the positive expression of love. So the child, too, has to learn to include both.

Again the same holds true of all relationships. We all enjoy the familiar works of love—reassurance, tenderness, and companionship; but along with these goes the fear that the loved one may be lost through death or accident, or alienated in some way. When our fear is allowed to separate us from our love, it remains unincluded and unsubordinated and its power becomes more destructive. Everything the fearful one does drives his loved one away from him. If instead, he keeps his fear in tension with his love it will recycle the fear and turn its destructive but potentially creative energies into more love power.

Negative/Positive Interactions and Growth

There is always a bipolar, reciprocal love-fear dialogue between persons that must be dealt with if personal relationships are to grow. The interaction between the negative and the positive may contribute to the growing strength and diversification of our power to love or to act. Through this dialogue between positive and negative responses we may develop helpful rhythms of closeness and apartness, of intimacy and distance, that are essential to every love relationship. This pattern of intimacy and distance will be discussed further in Chapter 8.

The sad thing about many human relationships is that the participants become bored, uninspired, and dead to each other. This is due in large measure to their failure to include all the aspects of the relationship as a part of its normal agenda. Many people, for example, cannot "fight" with a spouse or business partner when need be, for a number of reasons. The word "fight" is easily misunderstood. Here it means the ability to accept disagreements as a part of life and a readiness to stand up for one's convictions, but with consideration for those of others. It requires a sense of identity and competence. Thus "fight" means the ability to stay with an issue until some sort of solution, compromise, or resting place has been achieved. This may be accompanied by expressions of feelings of frustration, resentment, and anger. Some think that the expression of hostility and resentment signals the failure of the relationship and therefore is to be avoided even when such conditions cannot be kept out of mind. Other people are afraid to fight, for fear they will lose the love upon which they depend, particularly when they have known this love only as they obeyed or agreed with the person who is the source of the love. Actually the obverse is true: the failure to "fight out" an issue is a failure to make all of oneself available to one's partner, and this holding back deprives the relationship and the partners of growth potential. How can one be accepted if one is not on occasion unacceptable (although we do not have to go out of our way to be unacceptable)? When our unacceptableness occurs, however, we should try to include it as a part of ourselves, and trust others to find ways of coping with it too. Perhaps their first response may not be very helpful, yet our response to their response and the continued dialogue may finally produce some changed behavior, and reconciliation with and acceptance of what cannot be changed.

Resentment and hostility are the negative part of our love, and our working principle states that the power of our love should include and subordinate the negative that is in us.

A friend of mine illustrates such a situation by his discovery about his role in racism. He puts it this way: "I have to accept my whiteness and its role in race problems. I don't want to be racist, but because I am white I am racist even though consciously I fight against racism. . . . In a way, it is a relief to come to terms with the fact that yes, I, as a white person, have my share in the causing of racism. Rather than rationalizing it, however, I am now free to deal with it." His love is trying to include and subordinate his racism with the hope that the negative will be changed into its positive, namely, equality for all men.

The same principle operates between persons. That is, I have a responsibility to use my positive to include your negative. I cannot have your love without including also your negative aspects. When I include your negative,

I am, through the mysterious chemistry of human relationships, often made much richer than if I had experienced only congenial expressions of your love.

Many people feel that it is wicked and sinful for anyone to have feelings of hatred and resentment toward
another. The situation really is not that simple. If I
resent and hate someone without the intention of trying
to include this response in a subordinate way to my more
positive feelings of love and responsibility for him, then
my hatred and resentment are sinful and wicked. People
glibly quote Jesus' saying: "Love your enemy." His word
cannot be interpreted to mean that one does not have
negative feelings toward another. In very simple words,
he is saying what I am trying to state here, namely, that
if my resentment and hatred of another is included in
and subordinated to my more positive feelings of responsibility for this person, I can truthfully say: "I love
him." Human relations become destructive when we
allow the negative to escape from the influence of the
positive, when we allow the negative to operate indepen-
dently of the positive, or think of the negative as being
separate from the positive. Or as Martin Buber puts it,
the "thou" must include the "it," since I am both a
"thou" (person) and an "it" (function). We must all
expect to be used ("it") but always in the context of our
identity as persons ("thou"). If our relationships are intentionally those of love and caring, then any negative
feeling or attitude will be included in the positive and
subordinated to it.

After an experimental service of worship one morning,
at our Institute, we asked the group members to state
their reactions to the experience. All the comments were
affirmative. To be sure that every point of view was
represented, we asked if there were not some negative
responses. One member of the group spoke up and said

that he did not like what we had been doing, that it was contrary to his training and his expectations. We could sense the stiffening of the group's attitude in relation to to this negative response, which meant that there was the danger that those who had positive reactions would not include the existence and the meaning of the negative.

We decided, therefore, to ask the group members to identify their feelings in response to the negative comment. There were the usual replies. Some felt that the member had been discourteous, uncooperative, disagreeable, tradition-bound. One member said he was interested in having the objector elaborate his negative reaction. This the objector declined to do, obviously with some embarrassment, explaining that he had said all that he had felt was necessary to say. He was then asked how he felt about being the only one to take exception to our experience. He explained that he felt uncomfortable and yet honest. He denied feeling discourteous or defensive. His expressed opinion merely stated how he felt at that given moment.

The question was then raised with the group whether we could not include the negative response in the positive one and make it a part of the total learning process, because when we fear and exclude a reaction we lose something. A free discussion between the participants followed, with the result that in the end a greater sense of trust was awakened. The man who had made the negative response finally was able to say that he felt that he had made an honest and important contribution to the process of our education, and the other members of the group admitted that without his contribution, our understandings as well as our relationships would have been deficient.

The negative response, in this instance, might have been the more responsible one in the sense that this participant expressed concerns that eventually moved us nearer to the realization of the personal and its truth. What at first seemed a negative response became positive because it was included and dealt with in this way. Positive responses are many times only the superficial responses of an unthinking majority, and although at first they seem positive, they are later recognized as negative or at least incomplete. The crucifixion of Jesus, for example, seemed like a negative experience, but when it was included and subordinated to the meaning of the resurrection, it was transformed from a destructive to a saving event. We thus learn that life is most powerful when it includes death as a part of it.

Another illustration gives added understanding to this principle of inclusion of the negative in the positive: I have a friend who lost his job because of some very creative work that he had done. Disillusioned, he was tempted to give himself over to bitterness and despair. He had been almost totally disregarded as a person, and the organization which he had served failed out of self-concern to acknowledge its responsibility or to be faithful to the purposes it professed. He recovered from his despondency and despair because he included but subordinated these responses to his faith and continued belief in what he had been doing. Instead of engaging in recriminations, he put himself in the hands of people who could help him evaluate his assets and resources in order that he might make crucial decisions based on an evaluation of himself as a person for his future work and life. He still mistrusts the kinds of bureaucracies which he had served for so many years, but he has not allowed his mistrust to interfere with the growth of trust in himself and in others, in his own future or that of others. He escaped one of the greatest dangers that a person can face, namely, the danger of allowing a negative experience to destroy or obliterate his hold on what was positive and thus block his very life forces. For when the negative is not included and subordinated, our potential for creative response is diminished or rendered unavailable.

Facing Complexity and Change

The principle of inclusion of the negative in the positive makes it possible for all kinds of miracles to happen, such as the transformation of liabilities into assets. The fear of others, for instance, can be transformed into a growing interest in others. The fear of being hurt can be changed into a capacity for ministering to the hurts of others. Everyone is familiar with the amazing compensations that a blind person can make in his power of perception through the use of other senses. Writers can transform the agony and travail of their own personal lives into literature that inspires and empowers their readers to grow and achieve in their own lives. We are free, then, to use the life force that is in and around us. If it seems to be flowing in a negative direction, we still can recognize it as a source of potential energy and realize that we have the power to transfer and use it.

We often ask how we are going to find the truth and the direction in the complexities of our various life situations. The answer seems to be that only as we are able to practice inclusion of various points of view and attitudes—and especially inclusion of the various positives and negatives of life—will we gradually come to the kinds of understandings that will become our guides for dealing with both complexity and change. To move from the realm of the personal into the broader range of social issues, we can see the effects in society of allowing the negative to dominate the positive.

Mass education, for instance, runs the risk of being intentionally impersonal, as the more personal concerns

of the student are subordinated by the impersonal concerns for subject matter, technology, and research. The
more personal concerns of the student as a human being,
such as his need for training in human values and in communication, his positive interests in personal and social
growth, are largely overlooked. This process of subordinating the personal aspects to the impersonal can
be seen as the negative dominating and subordinating
the positive. The more constructive student and faculty
dissent undertakes to reverse the emphasis, and seeks to
have institutional personnel make the personal a primary
concern, to which the inclusion of subject matter, technology, and research will be subordinated. There is great
value in acquiring further knowledge and increased technological skill, but they need to be included under and
subordinated to ultimate relational purposes in order
that their potential creativity may serve the well-being
and further growth of man.

The same adjustment is needed in race relations. The
impersonality of slavery is intentional and subordinates
the personal. The Emancipation Proclamation reversed
this in principle, but it did not affect the practices
of our society. Since then, during more than a hundred
years, the black man has not been acknowledged to be a
person in the same sense in which the white man has.
Again, because the impersonal has dominated the relationship, the only hope we have for improved race relations is to affirm the personal in action and in relations
with the black man. And all his other values must be
included in and subordinated to his identity as a person.

The guilt of racism, however, is not all on one side.
Blacks, too, have contributed to the existing situation of
impersonality and mistrust. In response to being ignored
as persons, some blacks reacted with riots, which were
enormous acts of impersonality with mixed intentions of

destruction and retribution, and without inclusion of anything positive in the relationship. The rioting was, therefore, a destructive act, not only for the rioter but for the community as well. The challenge to the community remains: how to react to such destructiveness. Will the community see it as a cry for help, or will they respond with harsher enforcement of "law and order"? If our hope is that the occasion for rebellions will be reduced if not eliminated, and a basis for the reconstructed relationship be established, we must try to sort out the negatives and the positives in race situations, include the negatives, and subordinate them to the positives. The future of our relationships, especially the future of our world, depends upon our ability to get the personal into focus as the field in which we know one another as persons in personal relations, so that all else that we may know about one another, positive and negative, can be accepted and utilized for a just and humane society.

Moreover, the personal includes more than the intimate, sentimental, or erotic aspects of a relationship. It must include also the objective scientific knowledge of man, of the processes by which he functions, the nature of his institutions and organizations, and the philosophies by which he lives. One of the weaknesses of the Christian religion, both Catholic and Protestant, has been its historical failure to acknowledge this. Christians believe that the first revelation of God was in his creation, which included the revelation of himself through human relations. Then, in the midst of that transition between the appearance of biological man and the man of the future, appeared Jesus of Nazareth, in whom Christians saw revealed both the nature of God and the nature of man. That revelation was eminently personal. His life cut across every institution and all knowledge. But when the churches began to think about his life and teaching, they gradually reduced its meanings into complicated propositions of belief and forms that eliminated its radical challenge.

Over the centuries this process of cerebration and moralizing has produced a state of mind, a set of attitudes, and a kind of behavior that has only a remote resemblance to the initial meanings revealed by Jesus. Knowledge about him has been substituted for relation with him or his spirit. He is proclaimed to be the Saviour; and yet when we teach children to be good if they want to be loved, the implicit message is that if they are good, they do not need a saviour. Thus, ideas about God have been made more important than a relationship with him. The spirit of love, joy, peace, and long-suffering has been crowded out by the spirit of competition, divisiveness, manipulation, exploitation, narrow-mindedness and bigotry, to the point where only a small percentage of the population of the world is attracted to Jesus, who embodied and incarnated the personal in the form of a love that is free of everything but its power to love.

The worship of the churches has also become subpersonal, with a denial of freedom, spontaneity, feeling, love, need, and other manifestations of the personal. This is illustrated by the resistance on the part of many church members to the personal touch involved in "the passing of the peace," which is part of the ancient custom. When a member or a visitor to a church says that he feels the church is cold and unwelcoming, he is saying that the church is impersonal and is denying the personal that it professes. Too many lay members, clinging to old forms of belief and practice, use religion to escape the issues and questions of life. As in the case of all other institutions, the hope is to be found in a leadership that has the courage to keep the focus of belief and practice on the personal, whether individual or corporate. The church was born to symbolize and embody the relational, involving men, God, and environment. The time has come for us to explore the relational powers that are available to us in all aspects of our life.

Our experience of government occasions the same kind of comments. Our government was founded "of" the people, "by" the people, and "for" the people, with its duty clearly to serve the people. The government of the United States was founded upon a revolutionary concept of human life, of man's place in the world, of his role as a controller rather than as a subject of government. In our own time there seems to be a general unawareness on the part of many in government that they are the servants of the people. Even in the founding of our government, Thomas Jefferson warned us of one of the dangers of government: it almost automatically pulls away from its duty to protect the natural rights of its citizens and becomes preoccupied with its own power and the problems of its self-perpetuation. He felt that left to itself, government gravitates to empty patriotism and tyranny, and so it seems to have happened.

The responsibility of government for the personal— service to the needs of its constituency—has not maintained dominance over the concerns of bureaucracy, the processes of election, taxation, and budgets. Instead, the original purpose of government has been subordinated to the purposes of self-perpetuation, vested interests, and endless committees. Its self-regard blinds it to the role it might play in helping men work their way out of a technological morass into a state of life in which human values once again might be available to human beings. Because government does not understand and employ the proper relation between the positive and the negative in its own operation, men and women become despondent about it and cease to trust it or its representatives.

This analysis is not meant to present a grim and hopeless picture, but to incite action by the citizenry to help realize the potential of this country. All institutions depend upon the power of the personal, operating through individuals who influence and reform organizations. Through the development of organizations that combine the power and resources of intelligent people, government can be influenced to subordinate its own bureaucratic needs to those of the citizenry. We can no longer depend upon "government" doing it for us. Like everything else, government left to itself becomes demonic. *We* are the government.

Our thoughts about education, race, religion, and government make clear how important it is for us to learn to keep negatives in creative tension with positive purposes. Obviously, such a purpose can never be finally accomplished; it can only be worked at. It is a never-ending task. It is the form which present and future struggle for survival must take. To repeat a thought from Chapter 2: our future evolution is now in our control. The question is: Will we employ inclusion for the sake of the movement of life toward a new and higher level of being?

The Negative/Positive Aspects of Death

Death is today an overarching concern for both individuals and organizations. Can anything be more negative than death? Life is its positive, and life in its fullest must include and subordinate death. First, let us think about dying as a part of growth. In order to grow, we must die to, or give up, something that we already have for the sake of something more that we want to do or be. A man, for example, will give up ("die to") some sure position and security of opportunity for some future value. He endures fears of failure, doubts about his judgment and wisdom, decreased income, deprived living conditions, in the hope of new possibilities of growth, service, or wealth. He is willing to include the deathlike experiences and subordinate them to the power of the greater life forces that call him to new levels of growth and being. Couples may surrender a present working relationship for a new and more fulfilling one. It will be necessary to experience fear, pain, dislocation, doubt, and even sadness at the loss of something that has value. If they will not die to the present good, they cannot have the future good.

The experience of dying in this sense is training for the experience of physical death. Our way of life is preparation for dying; and grace in dying contributes enormously to the quality of life. When each man comes to his own death, his attitude and behavior toward it will be determined by the way he has lived. If he has been an exclusionist he will fight death and die gracelessly and without hope. Death for him is a strange enemy.

The inclusionist, on the other hand, greets his own death as an old friend. He may want to go on living, but if death is approaching, he recognizes it as a part of life he has experienced many times before. So he accepts his death as "passage" from one stage of living to another. His faith is partly based on those encounters with life on the other side of the deaths he has already experienced. With this faith he can now face the final test. The commonly recognized stages which he may go through are these:

1. At first he tries to deny that his time has come. It is always hard for us to believe that we must die. Others? Yes. Such denial is a part of the assimilative process and gives us a chance to gather our resources for what we

have to do. This is the first step in life including and
subordinating death as a part of itself.

2. Astonishment is succeeded by resentment: "Why
me?" There is something insulting and preposterous
about death. It is an offense against life, a crime against
being. The Source of Life has betrayed us and rebellion
fills the mind and heart of the dying person. This is the
second step of life's inclusion of death!

3. This resentment is then followed by an attempt to
prolong life, to bargain for the staying of the execution
of the sentence. Sometimes a person may hope that if
he is "good" and cooperative, the threatened end will not
come as soon. Here again is life's struggle to include
death by outwitting it.

4. Now the struggle of life to include death becomes
more fierce and takes the form of depression. There is
positive value in this phase because the person is weigh-
ing the fearful price of death and preparing himself to
accept separation from everyone and everything he loves.

5. Having accepted the price of acknowledging death
as a part of life, he becomes calm and compassionate
toward those who will be bereaved. In one way or another, verbally or nonverbally, he will say: "I am ready
now and am no longer afraid." Thus in final human
form, life has included and subordinated death; and his
faith is that out of this act of inclusion a resurrection
of life will occur.

In this day of accelerating change, increasing complexity, rapidly shifting values, vanishing environment
and ontological choices, it is good to know that we have
available to us principles that can guide our thinking and
behavior. Inclusion is such a principle. The employment
of the inclusive principle of the positive in tension with
the negative will open doors to the future of human life
and its structures.

7. Bridging Chasms and Gaps

Sometime ago, in my reading, I came across the question: "Where is the friend I seek everywhere?"—a question which lives in the mind and heart of everyone. It has been pointed out that the average American sees more people in one day than a serf in the Middle Ages might have seen in his whole lifetime. Today we are so surrounded by people, boxed in, run over, and lifted up by people, exhausted and renewed by people, greeted and loved, entertained and shunned by people, that we seem to be suffering what might be called "people-itis," that is, too many people and the consequent effects.

Not only are we reproducing too many people, with the result that we are running out of space and air and resources for sustaining life, but people are also living longer. Even people who would normally die of natural causes are kept alive artificially by the medical profession, a practice that needs to be questioned. People are retiring earlier, too, and therefore looking for things to do that will either help them to "fill time" or find meaning. Then there is a growing number of people unable to find work and maintain their own existence. People are increasingly becoming the responsibility of other people; massive organizations of "other people" are necessary to ensure the conditions necessary for the continued living of others— social security, community funds, voluntary groups, for example.

There are different kinds of people. So-called white people (who are not really white), black people (who are not always black), yellow people, brown people, red people, people from different ethnic groups, intelligent people, stupid people, in-between people who are sometimes intelligent and sometimes stupid. Currently we seem to have confused people. All this peopleness affects relationships between men as individuals.

As I mentioned earlier, we have in our society some people who are in control of enormous amounts of knowledge and who spend their time increasing the fund of knowledge for which we have to be responsible. Our technology is already so extensive that it is producing change more rapidly than we can assimilate it. Yet all this knowledge and all this technology has not notably improved the basic quality of relationship between man and man. To be sure, there are improvements. In some ways we are more humane; and yet what was humane about dropping atom bombs on two Japanese cities, with all its consequent suffering, impairment, and destruction? We still have ways of suppressing and rationalizing our cruelties, as in the case of the Vietnam war. The use of the bomb does not stand alone. The occasions and the methods of inhumanity differ, but its effects on human relationship are always more destructive than we have any way of measuring.

Coping with Our Differences

Quickly, however, the opposite needs to be said, too. There is present in human behavior a power for building, a power for loving and caring, a power for healing and forgiving, a power for using our inventiveness and ingenuity for constructive and creative purposes, a power for transforming ugliness into beauty, a power for transforming pain into glory and nobility. There are many examples of the caring work of people, singly, in small groups, or on national and international scale: The Marshall Plan after World War II, the United Nations, the Peace Corps, the medical ship *Hope*, and many others. The question is, however: Which one of these potentialities for good will at any given moment is going to be expressed? What resources will be operative in society to steer human response in the direction of doing justice, of loving mercy, and walking humbly with one's fellow man, which is the only way in which one can presume to think that he is walking humbly with his God?

The difficulties experienced in man-to-man relationships seem to center mostly around the differences that exist between men. There are differences of race and sex and religion and abilities; there are differences of education, talent, and resources; differences in interests and purposes; differences having to do with the space available to each for existence; differences of philosophy and life goals; differences between those who hoard what they have and those who want to share what they have. The list could go on indefinitely.

A few people, and these are inclusionists, are able to live out these differences in a complementary and constructive way. It is not always easy. There are often disputes, disagreements, struggles, resentments, but somehow inclusionists will manage to hold these differences in some kind of creative tension within the relationship. They may not be altogether happy about it, but nevertheless they are willing to try a complementary approach rather than risk rupture and polarization.

On the other hand, exclusionists make differences divisive. They take an all-or-nothing attitude toward who they are and what they believe in relation to the other side. They are afraid to risk a complementary approach, and often become victims of the destructive fighting that they precipitate. We can see these two contrasting attitudes sharply illustrated in the kinds of dissent manifested by young people on campus. Some of the dissent has been inclusive; some exclusive. The exclusionist approach, more often than not, has resulted in violence; the opposite may be noted where inclusionism was practiced as a basis for working out differences. The exclusionist in most cases made for himself a situation that became impossible and intolerable; whereas the inclusionist usually improved his, because he succeeded in building a wider basis for dialogue.

The Differences Between Generations

A further illustration of this may be seen in what is commonly called "the generation gap." This particular problem-situation can be useful in helping us to understand and respond to any problem arising out of differences among men. Some youthful rebellion may be mindless and engaged in as an end in itself. But much of it is an earnest, even if misdirected, search for meaning, for competence in the use of technology in support of life, and for a humanism appropriate to a technological age. But in spite of the grim picture, which unfortunately gets played up too prominently in the news media, there is far more communication between the older generation and the young than has been assumed to be the case. We read mostly about the noisy minorities, but even they are beginning to break down into splinter categories that makes generalization about them unsafe.

Some authorities say that eighty percent of our youth are responsive to their parents and follow the traditions in which they have been raised. This also, of course, can be a source of concern because it is not at all clear that the traditions of the past are going to be equal to the challenges of the future. Other parents, more liberal than those just mentioned, help to free their children from the domination of moribund traditions and to establish in them an openness to the possibilities that the new age presents.

Incidentally, the gap often seems to exist more between those under thirty than between the under- and over-thirty groups. My daughter, who is twenty-two, and my son, who is twenty-eight, belong, it would seem, to two different generations with entirely opposite points of view on the same issues. Then there are the differences that exist between youth of the same age, but with different purposes in life. The gap, for instance, between the technically oriented young person and the liberal arts student can be great indeed. Here, too, is need for the practice of inclusion because, as we have already indicated, the technologist needs to be in dialogue with the philosopher, and the philosopher in dialogue with the man of affairs. The age of increasing specialization has its dangers, and such specialization can become a barrier to communication in our society. The sturdier and higher the barriers of specialization, the less the communication, and the greater the danger there is to individuals, corporate structures, and the future of man.

In spite of evidence to the contrary, there are a great many families that pull together and enjoy each other although within the family there are differences. Many young people have developed a solid, healthy sense of identity because of their relationships with parents who, despite their confusions, nevertheless offer their children much in the way of personal strength and resourcefulness. Parents who have not outgrown their adolescence and are confused about their own identity and purpose in life, inevitably transmit to their young the same sense of aimless existence, with the result that both resort to substitutes for authentic living. As I have written elsewhere, parents are the anvils against which young people hammer out their own personalities, and it takes a certain amount of strength and endurance to be an anvil. Parents who are so immature that they cannot be patient while children work out their legitimate immaturity are a liability in any culture; on the other hand, when a child senses love and care on the part of his parents, it is surprising what that child can survive in the way of parental impatience, lack of wisdom, selfishness and sheer stupidity. Some parents mistakenly push their young people to exercise independence and make decisions before they are ready. This laissez-faire sort of approach, usually with no structure or an inconsistent one, is disastrous for the young person in the process of formation.

Many parents, however, even though bewildered, are making a desperate attempt to try to understand what is going on in the minds and hearts of their young people. As I have said before, I am living in a world vastly changed from that in which I was born. My children, however, were born into this new world and they have experienced it and understand it from within, as I cannot possibly do despite my studious efforts to grasp its meaning. We must, therefore, hear our children and even be

instructed by them before we make decisions and provide
the kind of guidance that young people need from their
parents. This does not mean that parents either abdicate
their role or force children to assume the parental role
in relation to themselves. That would lead only to disaster.

Two things at least are clear. Thoughtful young people
—those upon whom our future depends—rightfully question the "establishment," which here simply means
"things as they are." This questioning of the young is
their contribution to the dialogue between the traditional
and the contemporary. To be sure, youth are not the only
contributors out of the contemporary, as there are members of the older generation who too are capable of being
critical of our forms and institutions. We must be sensitive to the contribution that young people make through
their questions. The value of their "answers" may not
be equal to the value of their "questions"; but even their
attempts at answering their own questions should be
taken seriously, responded to honestly, as a part of the
dialogue that will guide us into the future.

Listening Across the Generations

Moreover, the older generation does not have all the
"answers" that they think they do, because they are not
asking the right questions. Therefore, it is out of order on
their part to "lay down the law" to their young. On the
other hand, it is true that parents, especially the thoughtful, evaluative ones, have learned something from living.
They possess perspective, possibly a wisdom regarding
the complexity of human situations that is often missing
in the young. Parents also may have a long-term view
about the nature of life, which if judiciously related to

the present can be of enormous help in complementing the contribution of youth.

To generalize on the basis of these observations, we would conclude that the first obligation of those on differing sides is to become aware of the resources available to each; and second, to be aware that their first function is to listen to each other. Only by the hard work of listening do we earn the right to speak, a right which is taken too much for granted. Speech is a gift, but not a free one. It may be conferred by others only in response to our free gift of listening. Youth are "driven up the wall," so to speak, when they are not listened to, when they are not allowed to think their own thoughts in the terms of their own meanings. But when they are allowed to approach questions out of their own meanings and terms, some very wonderful things can happen. I remember meeting with a mixed group of adults and late teenagers, and as part of the program, I had asked them to make two lists of symbols representing certain meanings to them. One list was to be of traditional symbols, such as the cross, the flag, the baptismal font, money; the other of contemporary symbols, such as long hair, jeans, credit cards, drivers' licenses, and the like. I then asked them to identify, where possible, a traditional symbol with a contemporary or vice versa. I was amazed and delighted to have one of the young people connect the credit card with the baptismal font. The correspondence of meaning that he saw was that the font also represented an unearned credit. That certainly is the meaning of a credit card, and it certainly is the theological meaning of baptism, in that grace is conferred without our having done anything to deserve it.

This way of approaching meaning developed a profound religious discussion between young and old which might not have been possible from a consideration of traditional symbols and meanings by themselves. Furthermore, the older people enriched their belief and acquired a deeper meaning of its significance in their lives as a result of the contribution that a youth suggested. In order to win these benefits about which all were enthusiastic, it was necessary for both young and old to offer each other the best of what they had, to give the other the gift of listening, and then to deal openly and honestly with what they heard from both sides. Out of this exchange emerged a relationship and an enriched content that neither side could have produced by itself. Furthermore, both a younger and an older person made the comment that they were impressed with the importance that skill (having the group list symbols and compare meanings) had on the use of knowledge (symbols and their meanings for each generation) in the achievement of relationships across boundaries (differences of age and attitudes). Indeed, all education needs to include this equal, rotating emphasis on knowledge, skill, and relationship.

Recently *Time* magazine (August 17, 1970; p. 37) had a feature account entitled, "When the Young Teach and the Old Learn," in which were cited the family situations of some public men that are excellent illustrations of the practice of inclusion:

'Democratic congressman Thomas P. ("Tip") O'Neill, fifty-seven, of Massachusetts' Eighth District, has good reason to heed the young. His house in Cambridge teems with five concerned children, aged eighteen to twenty-six, plus a constant dozen or so of their friends, all forever debating political issues. "At our house," says Susan O'Neill, a twenty-three-year-old teacher, "you sit down to dinner and get up two hours later." Her father "always asks our sources, where we get our information, how reliable it is." A few days ago, the O'Neills had a long discussion about hair. The congressman duly assigned an aide to do some research. "We discovered that since the time of Christ, the male species has worn long hair and beards about 90% of the time. The Western world turned to short hair and clean-shaven faces only after the Prussian victory over France. All the great heroes of America have worn long hair. It is nothing for Americans to get alarmed about."

'What makes O'Neil listen extra hard is the fact that he represents not only working-class voters but also 200,-000 students on thirty-four campuses in the Boston area —the most collegiate district in Congress. The Johnson administration got its early support on the Vietnam war. Then, in 1967, O'Neill made a hawkish speech at Boston College, his alma mater, to a hostile young audience that included two of his children. Irked by one student questioner, he exploded, "I've had forty-three briefings on the war from all the experts—Johnson, Westmoreland, Abrams, Bunker, Lodge, Rusk, McNamara—and I think I know more about the subject than you do." Replied the student, "Have you ever been briefed on the other side of the issue?"

'Later his children besieged him with antiwar arguments. Back in Washington, O'Neill interviewed top officials off the record and found all of them privately opposed to the war. As a result, he took the then "lonesome" step of breaking with LBJ and became the first outspoken dove among the New England congressmen. He has not wavered. In a recent House speech, he urged his colleagues to "change the perilous course of this nation." And he added, "Truly my children awakened me three years ago to the realization of how great the concern is, how deep the love of country and the desire to protect it."

'O'Neill's children have converted him on other issues: against the SST, for the eighteen-year-old vote. He blasts campus violence as a sure way to anger Middle America, a theme he pounds in campus speeches. But rational dissent is something else: "There is no comparison with the knowledge of this generation and that of my own at that age." '

Often the eccentric behavior of many youth is a distinct threat and distressing challenge to their parents; yet the enforcement of the law-and-order principle alone is not an adequate response to the threat that the parents feel. One thing needs to be kept in mind: the superficial significance of conduct is not necessarily the real meaning. All behavior has meaning, and usually the meaning lies beneath the surface and is not readily apparent. Young people who have been cured of their drug addiction report that drugs were not the reason for their having been addicted. Drugs were only symptoms of something deeper in the person or his situation from which he was running. If it were not drugs, it would be something else. There is nothing new about this insight into symptoms in relation to meaning, but we are seeing it in a new form with drugs. The reason for inclusion, and the practice of dialogue as a part of the technique of inclusion, is to get at such underlying meanings. When these are uncovered, it is often discovered that people who seem to be operating out of different points of view have more in common than is generally thought to be the case. It is only when we become exclusionists and base our responses on the rejection of differences at their face value that we run into serious trouble.

There is no doubt that much of the behavior of large sections of the population, older people as well as young, is hard to accept; but there is a reason for it, and if we are to have a future, we must find and relate to that reason. Young people's use of drugs, their casualness about sex practices, their repudiation of authority, their iconoclasm in relation to the sacred precepts and practices of the generation that produced them are not to be tossed aside as mere eccentricities or empty rebellion. They are the symptoms of a crisis which may not only continue but can get worse.

Knowing and Trusting One Another

People, to be sure, become problems for each other and get in each other's way, but they are going to have to learn to help each other and accept these differences and conflicts as part of the daily diet of life. Obviously this is not going to be easy. Most of us find honesty with each other very difficult to achieve. Too often we simply act out roles that we think are required of us and are afraid to let even our best friends know how it is with the inner man. The recommendation here is not that we wear our inner life on our sleeves and divulge all that dwells within us. Rather, the recommendation is that we should learn to be more open and honest about what we think and how we feel.

No virtuous person is all virtuous and without sin. Theoretically, we all agree with this observation, but in practice few of us apply it, with the result that we drift into illusions about each other, and become pretentious about ourselves. Under these circumstances, it is impossible for us to be moral or maintain the perspective and balance necessary for being truly moral. Without such perspective it is difficult for us to have trust relationships between man and man. A trust relationship, however, does include experiences of betrayal of trust or of mistrust. A trust relationship is one in which the quality of the relationship is such that the participants in it are able to deal with whatever happens, whether it confirms or contradicts the trust. The husband and wife, for instance, who are willing to risk their relationship to find each other, sometimes even in the face of evidence of mistrust, stand a good chance of building a basis of solid trust. To be sure, it is a risk, but what is the alternative that offers any kind of future, except to run away from each other, seek out other partners in which the tragic drama of mistrust may again run its course.

Another requirement of our relationships in life, although often absent in our dealing with each other, is our need to remember that no one of us knows another person as he is. We only know others from within ourselves, as an outside "event" existing from a "center" different from our own. Three people's experience of a person will, on inquiry, produce as many different "views" of him. If we could only remember this, our relationships would be less complicated. Instead, we make the mistake of thinking that our understanding of others is complete and accurate. But such understanding of a person is never possible because there is always more to the person than he manifests, more perhaps that he is yet to become, because of the growth process in which he may be engaged.

This failure to recognize the limitations of our subjective views of one another produces endless tragedies. We sometimes say, "Oh, she's just neurotic," or "He's stupid," and thus write the person off as a liability, without any potentialities or future. Nor do we realize that the little that we subjectively know may be due to our unwillingness to explore these very possibilities. Thus we live only on the threshold of our relationships with each other, and never penetrate the wonder, excitement, and mystery of the potential relationship.

An inclusionist seeks always, under all circumstances, to develop, "to grow," his concept of others, realizing that his subjective view of the other is always incomplete and partly erroneous because his perceptions are limited and biased by self-concern. A wife, for example, is an outside event, and her husband's perception of her is something that he has grown within himself, partly influenced, of course, by her thoughts, feelings, and actions in relation to him and others. Her husband is also a "growth" in and by her, fed by what he is and does. To the extent that we men seek to grow each other, the image we have of each other will more nearly correspond to what each is. The white man must "grow" his black man; the black man his white; a husband "grows" his wife and she "grows" him and the increase deepens and makes more rich their appreciation of each other, so that the potentialities of their relationships may be realized. We need to include the unknown in everyone: the not-yet-happened part of a person. It is there waiting to happen, to be born in response to the beckoning and encouragement of another.

Another major cause of exclusion and alienation between persons is the presence of guilt. Many parents, for instance, feel guilty about what they have done or have not been able to do for their children. Because of their need to be right and always to be in control, they find it difficult to accept and examine this guilt. But examination of guilt is important because very often we feel guilty about the wrong things or for the wrong reasons. And why should we feel guilty now when we are older and, we hope, wiser about something we did when younger and less experienced? On the other hand, when we are rightly guilty of failure, misconduct, or defensive motives, we find it hard to accept the guilt and make it part of our agenda for growth. Here is an instance where our deficiency needs cause us to be defensive and to practice exclusion in the form of blaming others, often our children, for our failures. If we can accept our limitations and guilt and try to learn from them, then we shall not have the need to be defensive about our actions or to make others responsible for our sins. This same dynamic operates in any relationship between man and man, as for instance, between black and white.

The focus of the problem of guilt is self-rejection, and self-rejection in response to guilt occurs because the guilty person is not able to include the benefits that derive from the positive aspects of sin. The honest and thoughtful person is able to realize that human goodness is never without some evil in it, but most of us are not used to thinking that in human evil there can be some good. The evil that men do is called the demonic or "dark side." A helpful analogy is that of the spacecraft in its flight to the moon when it moves into the dark side, and we are anxious about its reappearance. Each of us has a dark side and there is always a question as to whether we will be able to "fire the rockets" that will get us back into right relationship. When we go into the dark side of our relational orbits, we do take our creativity with us, for the demonic is the destructive expression of that creativity. Sin, then, contains a part of our creativity which is potentially good, but we need to have that restored to us, reunited with the rest of our power of being. Therefore, we should keep in mind and affirm the positive aspects of sin. This kind of understanding is implicit in our Lord's statement to the woman who was drying his feet with her hair, when he said, "Because she has loved much, she will be forgiven much."

Human relationships would be easier and greatly enriched if the mixed nature of our motives and behavior were better understood and accepted. For example, we esteem self-actualization but often fail to realize that it entails a certain amount of self-aggression, which inhibits care for and consideration of others. Our culture frowns on adultery, and yet it is perfectly possible for enabling love to be given and received in such a relationship. Racism has implicit in it a struggle for identity, although the means chosen to realize it—such as riots and segregation—may be self-defeating.

Inclusion of all the meanings of an act, both positive and negative, helps us avoid chronic self-condemnation and makes it more possible for us to accept and affirm impulses, feelings, and meanings that are sound and good, and on which we can build. There is one danger, however, the danger of justifying and continuing destructive behavior by rationalizing it on the basis of the positive aspects of our behavior. Illustrations of this sort of thing can be found, for instance, in the case of a local political candidate who advocates a strong conservation program, yet turns out to be board chairman of one of the country's worst polluters. In another instance, a newspaper reporter assigned to do a feature on sources of pollution, exposed some sacred cows; and as a result of his faithful reporting, he was fired from his job. In each case, guilt plays a destructive role and sets man against man.

Obviously what is needed is some kind of dynamic by which we can be more accepting of the complexities of the human situation and the vulnerabilities of the people who participate in them. The Christian religion, for example, is supposed to be Good News, namely, that the supreme act of love on the part of God in Christ accepted our duplicity and sin, showed us how to respond to hostilities and defensiveness, and unlocked the door to the possibility of all that we were created to be. Although crucified because people could not accept his love, Jesus responded, "Father, forgive them." Even hostility to love and defensive responses can be forgiven by love! If the truth of such acceptance were more fully realized, then we would feel less need to be as defensive about our mixed motives, duplicity, the "sin" mixed in with goodness. But somehow the wonder and the release that Jesus' example points to has been lost to us.

Yet nothing should stand in the way of its recovery— neither individual or national pride, nor the dubious privilege of being right, nor the maintenance of a morality which must always be tentative and relative, nor the status quo, not even the preservation of our present understanding of who God is and what he wills. Many a leader who thundered forth about what he thought the will of God was in a particular situation has turned out to have been a false prophet. The only will of God that anyone can be certain about is that he wills men to be and to be in relation. This truth is implicit in the new commandment: Thou shalt love the Lord thy God with all thy heart and soul and mind, and thy neighbor as thyself. Therefore no one, black or white, parent or child, Soviet or American, has anything to value above the value of a caring, creative, future relationship with each other. Obviously, these kinds of relationships cannot be achieved without suffering, without periods of confusion and doubt, even of real conflict. Thus the highest morality of behavior for us will be the morality of inclusionism, which seeks the unity and meaning of all life and excludes other points of view and values only as a last resort, but never excludes the relationships upon which life depends. An excellent illustration of this principle was expressed by the teenager who said to his father, "Gee, Dad, just because I have contempt for your politics, social standards, religious beliefs and moral code, doesn't mean I don't like you. I really like you a lot."

8. Free to Be Male and Female

The images and roles of the sexes are changing. Men can be weak as well as strong, and women can be strong as well as weak. They can look alike or different. Unisex or sexual difference is equally in vogue. Our views of our sexual identity and its roles, however, have been so culturally and religiously conditioned that many of us are too rigid to cope with the vortex of confusion that characterizes present sexual behavioral changes. Many men and women do not know what to think or how to act in relation to their own and the other sex. At one extreme are those who have thrown over all the restraining concepts and values that had governed sexual relations; at the opposite pole are those who maintain that the only answer to the problem is suppression and the enforcement of stricter laws, because sex is such a powerful drive that the only way it can be controlled is from without. The fallacy of their argument is, of course, that it does not work. The fallacy of the practice of the free-wheelers is that their license creates even more chaos and bewilderment.

Justice for Women

The Women's Liberation Movement is a symptom of the problem as well as an attempt to deal with it. Some of the extreme advocates would like to obliterate the differences in the name of what they call "equality." Unfortunately for their aim, there is no such thing as equality among men. There is no equality between males, whether it be anatomical, physiological, intellectual, occupational, or situational; neither is there equality among females.

Why then should we expect equality between male and female? Here again we run into the problem of differences that we have met earlier. There are differences, and they have to be accepted. Of course, some of the feminine liberationists maintain that there are no differences other than culturally induced ones, but more responsible observers and interpreters say that there are undoubtedly genetic differences that have to be reckoned with when working out the roles between men and women.

Unquestionably there are injustices in the situation of women, due to prejudices that have been maintained by both culture and religion. In the view of successive cultures, to be a woman has not been deemed an honor. This attitude has been fostered by the myths about the superiority of the male in relation to the female. Discrimination against women is undeniable. The time has come when certain changes must be effected. There is no reason why a woman should not receive equal pay for equal work, or be given a chance at jobs that are traditionally reserved for men. Educated women are capable of holding down such responsible jobs as president, members of the Supreme Court, members of the country's legislative bodies, cabinet members, church leadership, corporation executives. Allowance would have to be made, of course, for the biological function of child-bearing and -rearing (unless, as some suggest, eventually this process will be taken over by some kind of technological process that no longer requires the body of a woman). Without question, provision ought to be made for wider availability of abortion at the request of the woman and the consent of the doctor; and child-care centers should be provided for women who want to study or to work.

These three or four radical changes are going to produce unbelievable changes in the style and manner of family life, and they have already begun to do so. The question is: How accepting of these changes will we be and how adaptable?

Help for Men

The present situation is not good for men any more than it is for women. At the present time, men are just as confused about their role as men, as women are about theirs as women. While the Women's Liberation Movement is on the march and efforts are being made to do more about women's situations, there is also the male side of the problem. Men are confused about being men, about women being the power behind men, about women's emasculation of men and the loss of their psychological and physiological potency. The stresses and strains of men living in relation to women are considerable, because a man does not understand his own sexuality, much less that of a woman.

We are a people generally out of touch with our feelings, although living in a culture that deliberately stimulates feelings. Human relations provoke feelings. We have all these feelings and we do not know what to do about or with them. Men particularly think it is unmanly to show feelings. Because feelings are energy, if they are not expressed in one way or another, they turn in on the person and attack his body. The inevitable strains between men and women produce feelings that couples do not deal with. The home, instead of being a place of rest and healing, becomes an added source of destructive tension. Consequently more men suffer from stomach and heart and other physical disorders, and often die earlier than women; many of these men are the victims of their own undealt-with feelings. Men often joke about their relationships with women, but underneath the joking is a seriousness that betrays a bewilderment that eats away their identity, as well as the linings of their stomachs.

Furthermore, men suffer from a helplessness, an inability to care for themselves, not only physically but emotionally as well. Many men also are engaged in a kind of work which they do not like. Because of family responsibilities and preferences and demands of wives and children, men often feel pressured by what they consider exorbitant demands upon their earning power. These demands block their ability to engage in study that would make it possible for them to switch careers.

Another and very profound condition of the male that needs to be taken into consideration during these years of reworking the male-female relationship is the sexual fragility of a man. He is not as strong or as dependable and unshakable in carrying out his sexual role as is a woman. More is expected of his sexual apparatus than of that of the woman. There are times, which can increase, when he cannot function unless the right psychological and physical conditions exist. Much of the unhappiness that women complain about in their relationships with men is due not only to what men do to them, but what they do to themselves and through themselves to men. It is true that a woman can make or break a man sexually just as a man in his way can break a woman. These insights are not offered as distractions from women's rightful claim for "equality" but offered as factors to be considered as we study and experiment with the respective roles of male and female.

Whither the Family?

Change also needs to be made in family life. Certainly the present state of family life is not reassuring, and so why should we not consider possible changes? The present man-woman conflicts have had a disastrous effect upon the family. The increasing divorce rate is a witness to the deterioration of male-female relationships. In this day of throwaway bottles and cartons that litter and pollute the environment, we have also "throwaway marriages" that litter and pollute the human scene. There is also the frustrated state of many marriages that do not result in divorce and in which the partners continue a life of misery together. Further evidence of family deterioration is the flight of the young from the home. Youth flee from the values that were taught there, from the parents who could have been models for their development, from the place where community might have been experienced, from the home that could have been a refuge from stresses and strains in the strenuous process of growing up. This flight often leads youth to alcohol and drugs, sex and violence, and many other substitutes. Added to all this is the problem with older people: many marriages are troubled and guilt-ridden because of inability or unwillingness to care for their aged, so that old people are turned over to strangers with whom they must end their days in loneliness and lovelessness.

The "sanctity of the family" in many places has become only an empty phrase. Even when the family remains intact, it may be completely lacking in sanctity. For many people, sanctity means dullness. Today for many the answer to dullness is experimentation, which has produced such phenomena as partner-swapping, communes, and extramarital relationships. These practices are not cited for approval or disapproval. They are examples of the need of some to examine afresh and experiment more freely in an endeavor to discover more adequate male and female roles. This experimenting is happening whether we like it or not; and there is no way to stop it. Education and religion could use their resources to guide and inform rather than condemn and alienate. Religion, for example, will have to give up its advocacy of sexual suppression as the panacea for this problem. Education, on the other hand, will have to realize that there is more to sexuality than sex hygiene, techniques of intercourse, and the process of reproduction. Information is not enough. All people come with sexual apparatus, and when the time arrives, an instinctive readiness and ability to use it; but what they need is a maturity, reverence, wonder, and humility to guide and inform their employment of sex and to help them achieve the excitement of sexual experimentation within the framework of a supportive relation.

Increased freedom alone will not provide answers to the problem, because the question remains: For what will we use our freedom? Freedom, whether it be sexual or otherwise, is not a goal. Freedom is a point of departure, a condition in which we may make more responsible decisions. These decisions have to do with our responsibility for each other: the man's responsibility for the woman, and the woman's responsibility for the man. The first step against any discrimination, whether it be racial or sexual, is protest; but protest must lead to a more advanced and creative activity. There must be an acknowledgment of the discrimination on both sides and a willingness to risk dialogue in order to find solutions perhaps unforeseen by either partner. The "battle between the sexes" of itself can accomplish nothing.

The true equality of men and women lies in each being accepted as a person, deserving of the respect, assistance, and loving care of the other. Such acceptance should be characteristic of sexual experience even in adolescence. The process of growing up, as we have seen, is exceedingly difficult. The ambivalent forces within us both for and against growing are complicated by the outside influences of society that both encourage and discourage our movement forward. This is no less true in the area of sexual identity, function, and growth.

Sexuality is an area of human life in which we have the opportunity to practice almost everything that we have been talking and thinking about in this book thus far. In the first place, we have to choose whether our relationship between men and women is going to be one of exclusion or inclusion. Exclusionists, as always, are defeated in the beginning. For example, one man said that seventy-five percent of the responsibility for the marriage rests with the woman, meaning of course that he had only a twenty-five-percent responsibility for it. He is an exclusionist, with the result that his marriage is breaking down. In his case, he wants the privileges of sex but not the responsibilities for a full, mutual married relationship in all departments of life. In other words, he wants sex without sexuality.

Sex vs. Sexuality

What is meant by this distinction between sex and sexuality? Many people's thinking about sexuality is centered on genital activity. Our cultural and religious traditions have focused their prohibitive attentions on such sex activity as masturbation, homosexuality, incest, fornication, and adultery. Even intercourse in marriage has often been made a matter of uneasiness and guilt for both men and women. For many, marriage is only legalized sex. Not enough has been done to cultivate in people a more comprehensive view and feeling of sexuality, of sex activity as a creative power and a means of "grace." As a result, the sexual living space of both married and unmarried has been unreasonably limited. Traditional suppressions, especially those of religion, together with the explosive nature of the denied sexuality, have contributed to the current outbreak of free sex expression that has swung to the opposite extreme. A larger concept of sexuality is needed within which genital sex finds its expression.

By sexuality is meant the dimension of being that includes every aspect of the male-female relationship. Behind the distinction between sex and sexuality is the overarching matter of being human—both men and women are fundamentally and first of all human. What does it mean to be human? It means being incomplete and needing others; it means needing to give to others, to complete them and to be completed; it means growing and becoming; it means being frightened and defensive; it means withdrawing and returning to a situation; it means developing hypotheses or beliefs for actions the results of which cannot be foreseen; it means feeling and responding; it means struggling to communicate; it means having a growing value system; it means being a saint and a sinner; it means all that has been listed and more. But being human means being any of this as either a *man* or a *woman*, so that the dimension of sexuality is inclusive. In this kind of context the sex act is a profound source of pleasure and fulfillment and a crucial means of communication for bridging whatever gaps occur in the relation between the man and the woman.

Thus there is more to sex than "going to bed." Sexuality must include identity, difference, mutuality, and everything having to do with our total interpersonal relationship. For a woman it requires that she be aware of her femininity, to feel, to think of herself as a woman. Maleness is likewise a dimension, an awareness. To be a man is to become conscious of all that is unique about masculinity. Every relationship, whether man to man, man to woman, or woman to woman, is shaped in part by mutual awareness of sexual identity. Because I am a man I speak to another man in one way and to a woman in another way. So likewise a woman addresses another woman in one way and a man in a different way. Sexuality is always with us but sex as an act is occasional. Sexuality is more than a physical phenomenon, a device for reproduction, for achieving orgasms, simultaneous or otherwise. It is a vehicle of the spirit, a means of communication, a creation of community.

In response to this concept, as inclusionists we seek first of all to include ourselves in the relationship in order that we may include our partners authentically. How can we include another if we do not include ourselves? As inclusionists, therefore, we are aware of ourselves as male or female and are aware of the other as an opposite, which means that we are aware of the samenesses and the differences. Actually being inclusionists, we are thankfully aware of the samenesses and the differences, and this awareness frees us to build the relationship on what we have in common as well as on what distinguishes us as persons and members of different sexes.

The relationship between sexes has a greater potential for joy and fulfillment, or for misery and death, than perhaps any other. We are the two parts of creation: male and female. We are faced with the task of uniting creation, but each of us is faced with the mystery and difference of the other, and the incompleteness and loneliness of the self. We have two longings: one, the longing to know another; and two, the longing to be known by another. And yet ambivalence overshadows these longings. While it is true that we long to be known and to know, at the same time we are afraid to know and to be known. The fear to be known causes us to withhold ourselves, and at the same time to distort our efforts in letting ourselves be known. Our fear to know deafens us to the revelations of others, and also distorts what the other is trying to reveal.

Men, for example, are under the impression that they must always appear strong and aggressive, in control of situations, and cannot admit that there is another part of themselves that is tender, lonely, frightened, passive, and in need of care. What a man thinks are signs of weakness would contradict the image he has of being a man. When a man is unsure of himself as a man, he often seeks to reassure himself of his masculinity by acting tough and hiding his tenderness.

On the other hand, a woman has been culturally conditioned to present herself as one who is tender and loving, receptive, obedient, and compliant, allowing the man to be the strong and initiating one. She, too, has difficulty, however, accepting that she has another side to herself: that she has capacities for being strong, for being an aggressor, for taking the initiative, and possessing creative powers of leadership. When a woman is unsure of herself as a woman she may seek to reassure herself of her femininity by feigning excessive weakness and dependency. If the total capacities of each can be accepted by both, the relationship will be less demonic and destructive. The strength of women can complement the weakness and tenderness of men, just as the strength of men can complement the tenderness and receptivity of women.

The problem is how to break out of our misconceptions, embarrassments, and shynesses? Here, it seems to me, the role of inclusion is indispensable. Each of us must try to search the other out, firmly and with tenderness, in order that each may dare to let the other know how it is within us. The husband of a couple who were in serious marital difficulty finally made known to his wife, with the encouragement of a counselor, that his job was giving him great difficulty and as a result, he was frightened. She had known that something was wrong, and her attempts to find out only provoked him to irritation and defensiveness. When she learned, in the counseling session, what the real trouble was, she went over and held her husband's head in her arms, saying, "John, why wouldn't you tell me? Why wouldn't you let me know?" With that, he broke down and wept like a child. The love and tenderness that showed on the face of his wife was beautiful to see. When it was over, however, John was horribly embarrassed that he had wept and shown such weakness. Then followed a discussion between them about the full range of experience and feeling that both sexes are capable of, and how dependent a marital relationship is on the frank expression of these. Withholding in such an intimate relationship usually results in alienation and the development of patterns of pretense and cover-up. In the situation just cited, the wife said, "I want to be a part of all of your life, and I felt that you were shutting me out because you did not trust me." John said, "I did not want to overburden you. I have always considered it my job to protect you from anything that would cause you alarm."

Inclusion: Male and Female

The situation just described illustrates how important the practice of inclusion is. John had failed to include all of himself in his marriage. He thus prevented Mary, his wife, from including him. She was also prevented from including a very important part of herself, namely, her powers of endurance, strength, and reassurance in her relation to him. Both the male and the female are, each in his and her own way, strong and weak, active and passive, with capacities both to initiate and to receive. They should honor each other by allowing each to express both strengths and weaknesses. Failure to relate to each other in this way keeps the relation on a superficial basis, so that each, in response to his own incompleteness and loneliness, demands inarticulate help from the other without realizing that the other partner is also alone, confused, and defensive. There can be little awareness of the profundities that are involved in both the actual and the potential relation. Inclusion provides a way of living creatively and constructively with sexuality, which is the context for any specific activity.

Inclusionists are more capable of achieving a comprehensive sense of sexuality that leaves them free to explore the fullness of relationship with members of their own and the other sex. Expression of affection becomes more possible between man and man without fear of homosexuality; and between man and woman, whether they are married or not, without feeling pushed toward the bed. Fathers ought to feel free to express affection toward their sons, which their sons need long after their fathers mistakenly begin the more impersonal handshake relationship with their boys. Mothers ought not be afraid of expressing affection to their sons and fathers to their daughters. Withholding of affection has a disastrous effect upon the development of persons, and their capacities to relate to their own and the other sex. Men and women, generally, ought to be able to feel freer to express their affection when they greet and part from one another. There is no reason at all why men who are real friends should not embrace each other, even kiss each other on the cheek, without feeling that somebody will think they are queer. In other parts of the world—Europe, South America—the expression of affection is more common than here in America. All people, male and female, are psychosomatic. It is hard to express feelings of affection without touching, without the employment of lips, cheeks, hands, bodies. Yes, such activity is sexual but it does not imply or require specific genital activity.

Critics of this position may ask, "Is this not dangerous?" Of course it is dangerous—there is no approach to the relationship between men and women that is not fraught with some kind of danger. But can it be any more dangerous than the limited view of sex and sexuality that has prevailed for so many centuries? Everything that a man does can be misused, which means that it is necessary for him to achieve the capacities of relationship with some sense of responsibility and discipline for others as well as himself.

In the context of this kind of relationship, genital activity, where it is appropriate, is more meaningful than where it exists as simply an additive, unrelated to the full "being" aspects of the male and female. Sex activity apart from sexuality is what leads men to exploit women and to use them as sexual objects. Genitality apart from sexuality is what turns off women in relation to the sex act. Genital activity apart from sexuality is one of the reasons why men and women acquire habits of sexual response that result in the woman's becoming frigid and the male's becoming impotent. The separation of sex from sexuality is destructive to both men and women.

A part of sexuality is exploring the mental and emotional talents and abilities of each in relation to the other. Wise is the man who discovers that his wife has something to contribute to the areas of his responsibility even though she may not have the technical training that would qualify her to do his work for him. Similarly, wise is the woman who has the ability to accept the contributions of her husband in relation to her areas of responsibility. Not only is this a source of renewal, but it is also another way of each exploring and coming to know the unknown part of the other. Each should expect to be corrected and guided by the other, informed and reinforced by the other.

Exclusionist males seek women to fulfill their needs. They want to "make" a woman, that is, possess her. Exclusionist women want to control men, resent their demands, bargain with them for their favors, and are generally possessive. Exclusionists seek to buy a sense of belonging, and try to secure their "salvation" through bribes. Exclusionists are only aware of what is obviously present, either in the stimulus they perceive or the feelings already present in them. Inclusionists are aware, on the other hand, of the not-yet-happened part of the relationship, of the not-yet-experienced part of a mystery that will never be exhausted. Exclusionists either exhaust their relationships and have to change partners, or exhaust the capacity to respond to the meaning of sexual stimulation. Inclusionists are renewed, re-created, individually and corporately. Exclusionists fall into molds of relationship, into habits and patterns and ruts. Inclusionists, because of the freedom that they give each other, are able to explore possibilities with free bodies, open hearts, and experimental minds searching for the not-yet-happened part of their own relationship. Inclusionist males want to know their partners as women and who this particular woman is. As men they want to include in their knowing and experiencing what it means to be a woman. They "make" women only in the sense of helping them become, of achieving their identity as women, not only in relation to them but in relation to other men and women. Inclusionists explore the body and soul of their wives with joy and wonder; and the wives, being thus appreciated, are free to reveal and give themselves to their husbands.

And women, in their turn, approach their husbands with equal wonder. Who are men? Who is this particular man? They explore their husband's bodies and souls, and learn to rejoice in the revelations of what it is like to be a man, and take joy in completing their husband's being, in becoming the sheaths not only of their bodies but of their souls as well, and the renewers of their strength. In this exploration of their husbands, and in their joy of being known and accepted, they are completed and fulfilled as women. In this revealing and giving on their part, their partners are more fulfilled than they would ever be by demand and possession.

Thus union of male and female, at all levels, in all aspects of their relationship, is the work of inclusion.

Using the Power of the Positive

The relation between man and woman requires, as in every other relation, the ability to subordinate and in-

clude the negatives with the positives. The negatives of
disagreement, of misunderstanding, of unmeshed timing,
of isolating preoccupations, of false images must be included and subordinated by a love, a caring, and a trust
that is willing to labor and suffer through the pain of a
growing relationship.

We cannot assume that a union can be accomplished
without difficulties, which should be accepted as par for
the course. The success of a relationship is not measured
by the absence of problems but, rather, by what the
partners are able to do in working through conflicts and
achieving a new state of being and capacity for living.
The negative includes any experience that either party
has difficulty accepting. The approach to the unacceptable is to examine it for its deeper meanings, rather than
rejecting it without consideration.

Adultery, which is regarded by many people as a
negative experience in marriage, has meaning for both
husband and wife. There are at least two possible responses on their part. First, and commonly, is outrage
and exclusion of whatever is positive in the marital relationship because of the negative experience. Such is
the response of an exclusionist who cannot or refuses to
see the possibilities of including and subordinating the
meanings of the adultery to the possibly more powerful
meanings of the love between husband and wife. The
second possible response is to accept the adultery as a
part of the agenda of the marriage and strive to learn
and benefit from it. Acceptance does not mean approval
—we can learn from relationships of all kinds.

By way of illustration, there was a great moment that
most people seemed to have missed in the moral, immoral
movie, *Bob and Carol and Ted and Alice*. When Bob returned from San Francisco after having had sex relations with a girl there, he was unable to make love to his

wife, Carol. So he told her about it. Now came the moment of truth: instead of going into a rage and rejecting him, she questioned him as to what the relation with the other girl meant to him. When she found out that it was only a passing event, and realized that in telling her about it he prized his relationship with his wife more, she asked him if he had kissed the other girl. Bob replied that he had. Carol thereupon kissed Bob and asked, "Which kiss was better, mine or hers?" Bob, overwhelmed by the expression of her love and passion, replied, "Yours." And so on through the sequence Carol used the power of her love for Bob to deal with the more trivial and yet real meanings of the adultery. She used her love to heal and prevent further alienation. When he went to San Francisco again and was asked to spend the night with a girl, he returned home to his wife. Carol employed her love for Bob and his love for her to include and subordinate a negative force that had entered their marriage.

Inclusionists, therefore, are not so apt to be stampeded into negative responses by negative events. They look for meanings. They ask questions of themselves as well as others: "What does the negative mean?" "What need does it represent in the 'guilty' and the 'innocent' party?" "What can both learn from the experience and bring back to the permanent relationship?" When these kinds of questions are asked and discussed, there is very real possibility that the positive forces of the couple's love and care for each other will have the power to include and subordinate the negative aspects of their experience together. Exclusionists pursue a literal morality of law in relation to faithfulness; the inclusionist can be following a higher morality of faithfulness that embraces the total relationship, and is not so preoccupied with the meaning of the genital encounter alone. Morality, in-

cluding sexual, is rooted in our concern for the well-being
of our partner rather than in our own anxiety about our
purity or our satisfaction.

"Growing" Your Partner

And finally, relations between man and woman require that the man have the patience to "grow" his wife,
and that the woman have the patience to "grow" her
husband, and not allow their relationship to be cut off
prematurely by false assumptions as to who each thinks
the other is. To "grow your partner," then, is to both
nurture and joyfully enter into the unfolding of the
potentialities of the partner. This principle has particular
relevance for the relation between male and female.
Every person, by reason of being a unique and distin-
guishable person, is a mystery. Add to that the uniqueness of being male or female, and the mystery deepens.

Fred and Debbie met in college, and spent six excited
months getting acquainted with one another. They often
exclaimed how wonderful it was to find out who the
other was. They were married and quickly had to settle
down to the business of living. Fred went on to graduate
school; Debbie got a job. A year later they had a baby,
which they had not planned on. Life ganged up on
them. They began to take shortcuts to the solution of
problems, and in so doing bypassed exploration of one
another's needs and resources. The sense of wonder that
they once had disappeared, and with it the sense of
mystery and possibility. It was only natural, therefore,
for Debbie to come to a counselor with the statement,
"Our romance has disappeared." Actually, they had lost
more than romance. They had lost the one thing that is
essential for their continued growth, namely, a sense of
expectancy in relation to the other. Each had begun to
acquire a limited view of the other, and to think that he

had the other figured out, and therefore, to write the other off as a loss. They began to think in terms of having made a mistake and to resent their child. Each had fallen into an exclusionist trap with no possibility of a future.

Their task now is to realize that each is an outside, independent, lifelong "event," that each has only his private subjective version of who the other person is, and that his version is not completely synonymous with all that the other person is. The next step is to understand that each has to "grow" his own other. Fred begins to "grow" his Debbie, and she begins again to "grow" her Fred, and in so doing they begin to discover the not-yet-happened part of each other, the wonder and the mystery which they had not yet plumbed. For the first time, they explore each other's responses to the dilemma they had created for themselves, and each is surprised at the other's tenderness, suffering, resources, feelings of guilt, deep desire for something other than they had achieved, and each is touched by the sense of helplessness that they reveal to each other. The sense of helplessness that each had was largely responsible for the irritation that they manifested one to the other. As soon as they begin to grow each other, the quality of their relationship changes. Their power to cope with difficult situations increases. They learn to include the negative aspects of their relationship under the positive. Their fatigue and despair lessen and disappear. Their actions begin to anticipate things which have not yet happened in their relationship, which is a sure sign of the return of hope. This is what is meant by "growing" each other.

Some readers may have difficulty with this concept of "growing each other" and think it an egocentric, if not eccentric, approach to human relations. My answer is that we have no alternative. Yes, "growing another" is egocentric. Everything we do is from within ourselves. I have to be subjective. I cannot know you as you are; I can only know you through me, through who I am, through the only way that I am capable of perceiving and being. But is there no check on my subjectivity? Yes, in your "growing" me. This growth will become a mutual product in the case of Fred and Debbie as they achieve a relationship through mutual "growing" of each other.

Intimacy and Distance

The growth of human sexuality requires the practice of both intimacy and distance, indispensable requirements in marriage or any human relationship. The rhythm of intimacy and distance is a sign of health. We begin our lives in the intimacy of the mother-and-baby relationship, which is the cornerstone of personal being. Our experience of intimacy continues through childhood with increasing amounts of distance as we grow older. And thus the rhythm between intimacy and distance begins and should continue throughout the rest of our lives. The more mature we are, the more balanced are the two capacities.

Some people are afraid of intimacy, resist it, and finally lose their capacity for giving and accepting it. They are lonely and are apt to develop defensive behavior that only increases their loneliness and their uncreative distance from others.

Other people are afraid of distance and become insatiable seekers after intimacy, the constant intimacy that is suitable only for babies. They may also seek intimacy from all kinds of people indiscriminately, causing them to exploit others and be exploited sexually and otherwise.

When intimacy can be accepted, it unites and binds two persons into a relationship of mutual sharing and fulfillment. In intimacy the mystery and wonder of being is explored and revealed, and gifts of love are exchanged with an overwhelming sense of mutual blessing.

And yet withdrawal must follow; distance succeeds intimacy, and gives perspective and rest. It provides partners with the possibility of experiences with others that will serve to renew their primary relationship and their next experience of intimacy. When distance is experienced in the context of intimacy it has creative and constructive effects; otherwise, it is frightening and alienating. When intimacy comes in the context of an experience of refreshing distance, it is joyous and fulfilling; otherwise, it can be suffocating and cloying.

All of this means that partners in a relationship must learn to be open to growing together more and more intimately, but also ready to provide distance for each other. The possessive claims of intimacy often do not allow the partner sufficient living space to follow his own interests, to gain perspective in solitude, to relate to others and be renewed by them, and to gain his own identity. If the partners deny each other this freedom, this living space, they will destroy their capacity for intimacy and therefore their relationship. Gibran has a lovely way of expressing this in *The Prophet*:

> But let there be spaces in your togetherness,
> And let the winds of the heavens dance between you. . . .
> And stand together yet not too near together:
> For the pillars of the temple stand apart,
> And the oak tree and the cypress grow not in each other's shadow.*

* Kahlil Gibran, *The Prophet* (New York: Alfred A. Knopf, 1923), pp. 19–20.

Some Needed Changes

The principle of inclusion makes obsolete the need for the old authoritarian codes of sexual morality which dictated the same behavior for everybody regardless of age, time, place, circumstances, and motives. There is no dependable repository or base for laws governing the personal behavior of people. The appeal to the Bible, for example, as the basis of sexual morality is ridiculous because its different parts disagree on the matter. Neither is white American middle-class convention an adequate guide for a morality of the future. There has to be a better resource for meeting the sexual conflicts, changes, ambivalences, and ambiguities of the present and the even more disturbing ones of the future.

Inclusion is a biblical principle that provides a guide for sexual and genital behavior and makes possible a disciplined freedom for the formulation of new approaches to old problems. Inclusion, as we have seen, means being concerned for others, acting toward them with a sense of trust and responsibility. It means including oneself not only as a needy dependent person but as one who seeks to meet the present and future needs of others. Inclusion means accepting that people have feelings and passions as well as reason. It means having an awareness of the weakness, incompleteness, and imperfections of life and people and making a place for growth, retreat, regression, and even helpless arrestment of the growth process. Finally, inclusion means a capacity for compassion, healing, and forgiveness. It means being open to new possibilities for human relations—especially between man and woman—that would be humane and provide mutual lasting benefits not only for participants but for society as well. In this spirit we consider some alternatives to prevailing exclusionist attitudes toward the following problems:

1. Masturbation is common sex activity and is to be expected. The exclusionist moralistic view of it as evil is unsupportable medically and theologically. It is a morally neutral activity that is psychologically benign, and a part of the psychosexual development of every individual. Including it as such will prevent the development of unnecessary guilt that has complicated the sex life of millions of people.

2. The same is true for homosexual behavior. Every human being passes through what might be called a homo-erotic stage of development out of which he normally grows. Some people, however, remain in that state. It is an incomplete relationship, but laws making such behavior between consenting adults in private a felony are motivated by the spirit of exclusion. They inhibit rather than permit changes in behavior by homosexual persons. Inclusionists will seek to accept the positive (love) and seek to include the negative (incompleteness) for the sake of possible change and growth.

3. Exclusionist attitudes toward sex play, touching oneself and others, and sexual experimentation produce a disabling sense of guilt that interferes with the maturing of sexual development and responsibility. Inclusionist attitudes see such behavior as a possible resource for learning that calls for guidance and not prohibition.

4. In the past, sexual relationships were allowed only for those who were married, but this law is being seriously challenged all over the world. The fact that there are more women than men makes the challenge rather formidable. We need an inclusionist approach to the explorations of other possibilities for different kinds of relationships under varying circumstances. A study of anthropology and the history of different cultures re-

veals that men and women have lived together in all
kinds of relationships. There is, therefore, no reason to
believe that our present patterns will or should always
prevail. With the other changes that are occurring in our
society, we should expect man-woman changes, too. One
principle seems to be fundamental and enduring,
namely, that sexual expression ought to be appropriate
to the relationship of which it is a part. This, of course,
places a terrible burden on participants, because in
moments of passion judgment is impaired. This principle
of appropriateness and responsibility makes promiscuity
an immature, inadequate, and undesirable activity. We
have to affirm again that the sex act ought to be appropriate in the context of the highest values of sexuality
in which it exists. This standard requires that individuals
should strive for such a realistic awareness of themselves
and sensitivity to others that it would be possible to
understand and admit when a sexual expression is appropriate and when it is not. Therefore the door is open
to the possibility of premarital and extramarital sexual
relationships. In the interests of the persons involved,
these cannot be entered into irresponsibly or lightly, but
soberly and with a real sense of their responsibility to
each other and their future.

In relation to the single adult person, if we are to be
realistic, there has to be some other answer than ab-
stinence or sublimation. We need to explore new forms
of male-female relationships and, while affirming the
primacy of marriage and the family as the pattern for
heterosexual relationships, be able to condone a plurality
of patterns which will make a better place for the unmarried. The answers here are not clear. One thing seems
to be sure, namely, that sexual expression with the goal
of developing a caring relationship is an important aspect
of personal existence. But should it be confined to the

married and the about-to-be-married? Needless to say, alternatives to marriage present many economic and social problems which will have to be solved.

Interpersonal relationships between men and women can be altogether celibate and still be spiritually and psychologically rewarding. Thus celibacy is a valid option for those who adopt it voluntarily. Yet we should question whether society has a right to impose celibacy or celibate standards on those who do not choose them.

Finally, there is the matter of the relationship between male and female in other than familylike relationships, for example, between men and women who are colleagues in a profession or business. Both have to be on guard against what we might call their male-ism or their female-ism. An analogy will be helpful here. As a white man, raised in a white society in white schools, associating largely with white people, it is inevitable that I should become, even unintentionally, a white racist. And so likewise, a black man, living in a black society, raised in black schools, inevitably, even though unintentionally, tends to become a black racist. An so likewise, men, raised as they are in this culture, are apt to become male-ists and women, female-ists, with the result that they do an injustice to each other and enter into an exclusionist relationship. Both must practice mutual respect. Attitudes of expectation, willingness to explore the possibilities of relationship, readiness to accept resources in the other will help each to complement the other. Each must make allowances for the limitations of the other, and avoid as much as possible exploiting whatever advantage either has. Only in this way can there develop a complementary relationship between the unique gifts of the male and the female, neither of which is complete without the other.

Our future depends upon our relations between man

and man, and man and woman. Indeed, individually, corporately, and as a race our future depends upon it; and our fulfillment requires both biological and psychosocial mutuality. If there were more mutuality between male and female, the female might have the power to help the male to be less aggressive. Together they might then realize a peace on earth that has never before been achieved so that the human race could go on to a new stage of being and development. Working out a complementary relationship between men and women is an indispensable way of keeping alive in this particular aspect of a lively world.

9. God and Growth

For too many people, the presence of God has been hidden behind massive ecclesiastical and theological superstructures or buried under the accumulated rubble of systems long since found wanting—superstructures of so-called orthodoxy, church organization, and bureaucracy; the rubble of repressive morality, religious trivia, and exclusionist attitudes toward man and God. Although the more thoughtful of ministers and laymen are struggling to escape this situation and find anew the presence of God, there continue to be far too many people simply walking away from churches where God's presence is hidden.

The Jesus of the "here and now" kingdom of God, the radical who searched out the true roots of the relation of God and man, the teacher who regarded man's relation to man more important than subject matter and law, the leader whose consistent love theme broke the

Roman power through his nonviolent acceptance of its destructive power that executed him, is hard to find in the accretions of two thousand years of "Christian" history. Insofar as we have lost him and his inclusive power we have lost the power to confront the world.

Without his spirit the days ahead will be grim. The Vatican has retreated and dug into positions far behind those of Pope John. Courageous men are either imprisoned or live under the threat of imprisonment because their convictions disagree with administrations. Hate campaigns are well financed by interests that do not want the spirit of Jesus to get loose in the world. Commercial advertising appeals day and night to the most demonic impulses and needs in people: the vain, self-seeking, superficial concerns that keep them from discovering self-transcending and fulfilling reasons for living.

The churches' concern for themselves as institutions have made them a natural companion with all other egocentric institutions. Prefabricated God-talk and programs fail to come to grips with the real issues—fear, conflict, change, and ambiguity.

Clergy have been trained to give "God-talk" to their congregations, without having been first helped to understand the fundamental and profound questions implicit in man-talk and man-activity. The result has been that what ministers and priests say, both in worship and in preaching, makes little sense to laymen. All too often their message is defensive, dated, and not worth being heard. I write as one who has listened to the agonized accounts of bewilderment and struggle of over four thousand clergymen from both Protestant and Catholic churches. They struggle to find expression for their vocation as ministers and priests out of the dated formulations and the theoretical practicum that were given to them when studying for the ministry. They have been trained to serve in yesterday's church, not the church of today and tomorrow. The reason so many laymen have been lost is that many church leaders themselves seem to be lost too. The most alarming fact is that a religion which *could* help men to meet the challenges and changes of our time is not available. Small wonder that so many people go through the forms of church observance yet never find the experience of worship helpful in dealing with what they encounter in life.

A man whom I knew only casually greeted me one evening at a party by saying, "You're a lucky guy." I asked him how so, and he replied, "Well, you have something really meaningful to do. Through your writing and your teaching, you make a difference in people's lives." I replied, "Yes, that seems to be true, at least in some instances, but how is it with you? What is your feeling about yourself?" After a moment's hesitation, he replied, "Well, not so good. I am in my mid-fifties, my wife and I have raised our family, and we are proud of our children. We have a lovely home, and I have an excellent job as vice president of a corporation; but before I die, I wish I could do something really significant, something that would make a difference." Later he added, "I feel guilty, not only about what I have done, but what I have not done." After some further discussion, I remarked that I had often seen him in church, making use of the various means of grace available to any believer— listening to sermons, going with his family to the altar for Communion. I then asked, "Have these not helped you in any way?" He looked startled, and asked, "What have they got to do with what I am talking to you about?"

Here was a man asking fundamental questions having to do with his very "being," what we call "ontological" questions. For some reason the meaning of these questions had found no relation to his religious beliefs and observances. He said later that he realized that he had been living in two worlds: the world of his own deeper concern and the world of his formal religious observance. This split between "faith" and life is why religion and church have ceased to have meaning for a great many people. The failure to connect ontology with theology is one reason why religious leaders have lost their power to help people use the resources of religion in relation to their problems of "being." Many people have only a negative association with religion. They recoil from its bad taste, its righteous anger, its sexual repression, its bigotry, its spiritual pride, its preoccupation with inconsequentials. They experience it as just another responsibility, not as a resource for meeting other responsibilities; or they experience it as a source of condemnation, as in the case of a young mother who was told that God was punishing her for sins by making her child sick. Still others are repelled by what they regard to be the church's excessive involvement in social issues. Even thoughtful, earnest people who are not rebelling, but seeking earnestly for some help in their search for God and for ultimate meaning, are turned off by much that is offered them in the name of religion.

Obviously the contemporary church is not offering either to its members or to society firm leadership in these matters. It is not providing society with clear goals or the strength to reach those goals. It is regarded by many as so reactionary that it is unable to exert moral leadership in community life. Still others regard it as so progressive and way-out that they feel that it has deserted the "faith." And some are offended by what they regard as its oversimplifications of and insensitivity to life's complexities and issues. The purpose of religion and the church is not to indoctrinate members and to disseminate in society its own exclusionist doctrinal subject matter; nor is it to impose on society its system of morality or ethics, or on its members a form of worship to which men must be slavishly obedient. The purpose of the church is to enable a meeting of meaning between God and man, to help men to find their identity and their responsible relation to other men, and to achieve moments of soaring beyond the normal and usual levels of existence.

What Is the Task of the Church Today?

The religious task today, then, is not to defend the faith, but to translate it, to hear with it; and then, on the basis of what is heard, to respond to the responses and questions of a searching generation. Unfortunately, however, most church teaching, whether it be of adults or children, presents love, patience, forgiveness, and reconciliation as moralistic abstractions. Often ignored are the members' own struggles, conflicts, and alienations; their acts of vindictiveness and judgmentalism, as well as the other negative manifestations of men trying to live in community. But the full agenda of religion includes not only theology and doctrine, but life: the struggle of men to live together in both despair and hope and with understanding and love.

The story of Jesus' birth, temptation, work, trial, death, and resurrection is the original story that gave men hope, and was the basis for the forming of a group of disciples who were the forerunners of the "church." This group understood its origin, power, and transcendence over fear in terms of its relationship to Jesus. The story of Jesus is every man's story, but each person needs to learn to interpret it in terms of the meanings of his own life.

The repetition of the story of Jesus, without relating it to our own lives, can become so familiar and commonplace as to become trite. Therefore every person must discern within the meaning of his own living that which relates him to the story of Jesus and makes it *his* story. When he can tell his own story with excitement and conviction, he has identity, power, and a sense of being a part of a support group that gives him moments of soaring release from the ordinary and the mundane.

How does one translate the story of Jesus into his own story? Here is an illustration of how it was experienced and told anew in one group and for one man. A group of twenty-five people were asked to meditate about a small wooden cross that had been put in a half-filled wastebasket in the middle of the room. After a minute they began to respond both verbally and non-verbally to what they "saw." One person picked up the cross and held it high over his head as a symbol of what it meant to him. Another person put the cross under the wastebasket, as symbolic of the way he felt his living hid the cross. A third person put it back in the wastebasket as a reminder that the original cross was raised on Golgotha, the city dump. A fourth person said, "I'd like to get both cross and basket out of the way because they bother me," and he put them out of sight, saying, "I think our difficulty is that we depend too much on external symbols. Why don't we put our arms across each other's shoulders and thus each of us make a cross, symbolizing that the cross is to be embodied in human relations and in the organizations of human beings." Finally, one man admitted that he hated the cross. He added, "I wanted to destroy it. It makes me feel guilty and I want to smash it." When asked why he didn't do it, he said that he was afraid.

After a long pause a man who thus far had said little during the conference and who seemed unhappy and depressed, got up and went over to the person who was now holding the cross, took it, threw it on the floor, and smashed it with his foot so that its shattered pieces littered the floor. Joe, who had expressed this violence, stood a moment looking at the debris, breathing hard with his hair hanging down in his eyes. He returned to his chair still agitated. The group was simply stunned at first, but finally began to express concern for the broken cross. Joe was weeping silently.

This incident is symbolic of where the concerns of too many church people really are. We are more concerned about symbols, institutions, property, propriety, and doctrine than about what happens to people. When somebody asked, "Whose cross was it?" the leader replied that it was his, that it was made for him by a friend, and that over the years it had gathered much meaning for him. This information made them more concerned about the cross. Finally, one person said, "What about Joe? How does he feel? What does this mean to him?" Joe was still trembling, alone until this moment. Gradually they forgot the shattered cross and began focusing on the meaning of what was happening to him—his sense of isolation, of frustration; his need to relate if only through an act that others experienced as hostile; his fear of himself and others, his disappointment in the meanings of the event; his need to participate and contribute the uniqueness of his own concern. At last the cross became the symbol of some of the gut meanings it had originally borne. But the group—the church—had to forget the smashed cross and its superficial concerns for property and propriety in order to minister to Joe. Here is a parable for the church in relation to its opportunity in today's world. It must treasure what it has by letting it go, by letting the world deal with it as it must.

How did the event end? After much discussion and evaluation of what had happened and its meaning, the leader drew Joe to his feet, picked up a part of the broken cross, and holding it between them, embraced him. The rest of the group gathered around in support of the two figures. It was an experience of humility and exhilaration. The next day the leader found the cross repaired, sitting on his desk with a note from Joe on which was written, "Thank you for sharing your cross." For the leader his cross, though scarred, was more beautiful than ever. And so is the life of Jesus made more beautiful to the world by being embodied in our struggles.

The true business of religion has to do with the relational, and orienting men toward the new relational forms and modes for the most pressing needs of contemporary society. Exclusionists are antirelational and, therefore, antireligious, despite their possible religious professions. In setting up categories which separate men as good and bad, true and false, right and wrong, black and white, they destroy the possibilities of human religious response. Likewise, they become notoriously judgmental and unforgiving in their overwhelming need to be right. Over the centuries this strong tendency among churchmen to exclusionism has generated a series of religious struggles. Even in the time of Jesus, for example, scribes and Pharisees had multiplied the laws governing human relations to the point where they had become an intolerable burden; and, as Jesus said, these same people would not so much as lift a finger to help men carry the legal burden. Their law was exclusionist in spirit, dividing and separating men, Jew and Gentile, Samaritan, saint and sinner. They were more interested in the niceties of law and orthodoxy than they were in people as persons.

So it has been since. Historically the Christian church has been maimed repeatedly by outbreaks of exclusionism: the split between the Eastern and Western churches; the Inquisition, the Reformation, the division of Protestant churches into denominations that subdivided into still more denominations; the splitting of local congregations into separate bodies to multiply the confusion. The whole missionary movement was disgraced by the prominence in it of an exclusionist spirit, with the result that a very small proportion of the world's population became Christian. Even in America today, only half of the population identifies itself with any particular church. The exclusionism of many Christians has finally produced a condition in which most people have no respect for what the church claims to represent.

Christianity ought to make a lot of sense in relation to men's struggles between love and hate. It is disillusioning that instead of placing on its agenda the concrete problems of love and hate, anxiety and alienation, its emphasis has often been on obedience to law, the suppression of feelings and questions, and the exaltation of a superficial, conformist style of life and worship. But the existential life which this religious exclusionism denies, the life it disposed of by calling it sin, the same life that it was supposed to have redeemed, has now rebelled. The rebellion is an expression of the lost hope that religion has anything pertinent to say to it.

The Basis for Hope

There stirs, however, another spirit, the spirit of Jesus, who infuriated the "religious" people of his own time by his spirit of inclusion. Those whom they rejected he included. They complained that he consorted with sinners and publicans, the very people whom they excluded. He included himself by performing acts of mercy and compassion on the holy days when such acts were forbidden and those in need excluded from the concern of the "religious." He first included himself in the life of the people. He was able then to accept their life and their symbols of meaning, such as sower and seed, the growth of a plant, salt, yeast, a colt, the foal of an ass, and finally the cross, and by means of these he taught them new meanings and demonstrated new relationships. He built on their meanings to convey his own.

Yet Jesus had his moments of exclusion, too: he left a region where the people had no faith; and he drove the money-changers from the temple. But these acts of his were in the broader context of his outreach and inclusion, whereas the exclusionism of the Pharisees and publicans was their whole way of life.

Jesus' inclusionism opened up a new way of life, but his followers turned it into something that I believe he never intended, into a legalistic religion which is much less than what he himself portrayed. It took his followers only a few centuries to place men back in the bondage of religious law from which he had striven to relieve them. And yet in spite of legalism, churches have always nurtured in their life millions of saintly common people in whom the Holy Spirit has been revealed to men despite stifling religious structures. In addition to these common people, there have also been mystics, philosophical theologians, educators and other leaders who, over the centuries, sought time and again to purify and liberate not only the faith but the people who were trying to be faithful to the gospel in the face of so many obstacles, repressions, and discouragements.

An act of inclusion is an act of acceptance and love,

which means an act that attempts to bridge whatever separates man from man. Underlying all our many problems—social, financial, governmental, educational—is the personal, the deep concern with the human conditions in which men must live their lives. Basic human issues are money, jobs, education, housing, transportation, sex, movies, family life, drugs, alcohol, the draft, the war, peace, love, joy, fulfillment of the spirit. Religion arises out of the application of love, justice, and mercy in dealing with these issues. If anyone would find God, then he must include himself in these conditions; and there in the midst, work with other confused human beings, and employ all that is available to help society in the way of knowledge and technology. Thus is God to be found. Exclusionists would have religion concerned only with religion, and churches as ends in themselves. True religion is concerned with the total range of human life in relation to God.

What then is the truly religious person to include? First, he is to include himself in the life that surrounds him, not intrusively and offensively, but with careful concern for the needs and capacities of others. Jesus did not thrust himself upon men. He went where they were, he invited them to be with him, he accepted their rejection of him. He offered the best of his thought, the fullness of his feelings, and was unashamed of his weaknesses. He accepted the virtues of his integrity without either false pride or modesty. Whoever would be a follower of Jesus is called upon to match the words of his profession with appropriate, congruent feelings and deeds, and to be a participant in life in all of its manifestations. The human spirit is amazing. It refuses to be stamped on or to be stamped out. It prefers to create rather than to destroy. This is a miracle in the midst of the destruction that is all around us. It is the task of the church to affirm, feed, encourage and reverence such miracles worked by the human spirit. Men today are going through tremendous struggles. They are wrestling with their gods, and we who profess to be followers of Jesus are called upon to affirm them in their struggle and to include ourselves in it.

A religious inclusionist is more interested in the questions that men are now asking than in the prepackaged answers that any particular version of religion might have to offer. They believe that the Spirit is working in, through, and between men, and that those who would participate in the Spirit's work must learn to be alert to the questions that men ask as a guide to their response. The man whom I met at the party was asking three basic ontological questions about his finiteness, his search for meaning, and his guilt. First he said, "Before I die . . ."; he was concerned about his finiteness. Second, he said, "I would like to do something significant . . ."; he was concerned about meaning. Third, he said, "I feel guilty . . ."; revealing his sense of guilt.

Our difficulty is that we have not been trained to listen for questions. We are trained instead to give people answers. We need to realize that what we believe is something to listen with as well as to speak about. If we have a gospel, we are to listen with it before we speak it. With what we listen determines what we hear. When we approach people with a set of presuppositions we hear very little. Inclusionists who open themselves to people with a full awareness of them and a compassion for their search for meaning hear profoundly. Since hearing programs response, what we hear teaches us what to say and how to say it. As we noted earlier, hearing more often unites men; speaking often alienates them. A God-filled man is not afraid to hear; whereas a lonely man is, because he does not know whether he can handle the meaning of what he hears.

Men emerge from their experiences not only with questions, but with answers as well. They acquire insights and "answers" that have authenticity, which wise teachers and pastors may help them to relate to the universal truths discovered earlier in human experience. Here is another instance of how the listener unites men through response not only to their questions but to their answers as well. Exclusionists, unfortunately, insofar as they listen at all, do so competitively, divisively, and defensively.

Worship As Dialogue

The religious inclusionist opens himself to dialogue with the expectation that out of the exchange there will emerge either a truth or a new depth of meaning that neither he nor the participants could ever tap individually outside the dialogue. The exclusionist, on the other hand, is afraid of dialogue, partly because of his need to be right, but more often because of his fear of being proven wrong and having to abandon a position on which his security depends. A truly religious man is thus a growing man, depending upon his interaction with other men, either in face-to-face dialogue or through literature or some other form of communication, for the stimulus that produces the growth.

Religious inclusionists are aware of mystery, and the unexplainable and the unknown are neither an embarrassment nor a threat to them. They do not have to be in control of everything, nor do they feel compelled to be omniscient. They find excitement in mystery and stand in adoration of goodness; they are capable of

wonder and able to stand in awe of that which is beyond
their comprehension. They have a sense of reverence for
themselves, for other men, for issues with which they
struggle, for the truth which they know, for the truth
which they have yet to learn, and above all, for the Holy
Other, whom they call God, who stands over against
them, above them, and beneath them as well.

A primary task of the church is to help men and
women sort out and focus the meanings of their lives in
relation to ultimate and eternal meanings; and to stimulate, inform, and guide men in their dialogue with God.
This is its religious thing, its specialty. Many clergy complain that they do not have a specialty, and are the only
generalists left in a specialist society. That is only so because they themselves are trying to do everything as coun-
selors, therapists, group specialists, community organizers,
administrators, demonstrators—much of which can be
done as well or better by laymen and should be done by
laymen. Many business and professional people are now
saying that they wish the clergy would leave such action
programs to them and, instead, help them with the religious and theological meanings of their lives. This is the
clergyman's specialty and must be increasingly so, as we
move into the future.

A business executive, who also worships regularly, asked
me what connection there could be between his business
and his faith. During the discussion I asked him: "What
doctrine of man underlies your system of management?"
He was startled and, of course, he could not answer because the language of my question was strange to him;
so I changed my question to: "What kind of concept of
man determines how you run your organization?" He
explained that he did not expect much of his personnel,
that they needed to be directed and told what to do and

how to do it. He further explained that he and the few people close to him provided the creative thinking and innovative ideas for his organization.

I explained that his concept of his employees was his doctrine of man, and I asked him to compare it with the doctrine of God and man that he professed and expressed in his worship. Again he was startled, but he began a process of rethinking his concept that ultimately changed his way of regarding and treating his employees. He began to have confidence in and expect more of them. He has given them more freedom, responsibility, and the power of initiative, in keeping with the Christian view of man which he professes. His doctrine and his practice are no longer out of touch, but work together. This incident illustrates the kind of correlation that people need help in thinking through, and for which many people are asking.

An important focus for this kind of specialized task of correlation is, and will be, worship. Men will always congregate, and the more fragmented they become in the various aspects of their lives, the more they will seek in coming together the means of restoring their sense of wholeness, their sense of relationship to each other, and their sense of the Holy Other. The knowledge and technological overload that mankind is developing calls for a new sensitivity to the relational base of society without which the structures of our culture will collapse. Man's future depends on his capacity to use knowledge and technology to build structures of relationship that will support life as a benign and creative enterprise.

During the immediate decade ahead, which promises further specialization of human knowledge and technology, the church's potential for correlating new knowledge with the old faith and the expression of this in worship will be needed and, therefore, must be actualized. Much present worship, either liturgical or free, is not equal to the future task.

What Changes Are Needed in Worship?

Much worship is sterile because it is too cerebral and cuts people off from their bodies and their feelings. It is curious that an incarnational faith should have encouraged in its practice a separation of mind, body, and spirit. Much of its practice disembodied the psyche. Now we must work at re-embodying the disembodied worshipers. The body is the instrument of the person without which there can be no communication. People who recoil from physical contact or activity as a part of worship deny an indispensable part of themselves and a resource for communication. Most of them accept the body as indispensable in other parts of their lives. Why not, then, in worship? We believe (theoretically) that the Holy Spirit incarnates himself in man, individually and corporately. If so, he needs the whole of us. My hands, arms, face, legs, and feet are his; and if I withhold them from his use, what gifts of his may I be withholding from others? Why not then clasp hands with a pew neighbor, or even embrace or kiss him or her if appropriate to the relationship? Why not clap our hands before the Lord in tune with music or dance, and thus express the feelings of the soul? The incarnate Lord calls for incarnate people to worship him.

The thrust of worship must be toward the future. Too much of it is focused on the past. Instead of walking backward into the future with our eyes fixed on the Apostles, we ought to be walking through the present into the future with the Apostles at our backs with a faith that dares to risk an unknown future. Any worship that is less than this is not worthy of the God of history or equal to history's task. There is continuity in the relation of past, present, and future; but, there is discontinuity, too. We cannot expect, therefore, to have worship without change any more than we can go back to a world without change. Of course, there is fear, confusion, doubt, and despair, but our worship should gather them up as a part of our offering where they will be recycled and transformed into courage, faith, and hope. A worshiping church is now being called upon to act in anticipation of that which has not yet happened as well as celebrate the great redemptive acts that have already happened.

At this point, religious faith, the Christian faith, together with all other religious endeavors of man has special relevance. The forms of church life and worship will have to change. The question is whether our ecclesiastical and denominational egoism and liturgical traditions will allow us to respond to the challenge and make use of the obvious opportunity that has presented itself. How hard it is for us to remember and accept that death is built into every form of life that we know. Some part of us must die in order that the real part may not perish. So it must be with our worship forms. Moved by the Spirit, we hope, men made them; moved by the Spirit, we hope, men must surrender them and make new ones. But there should always be a creative tension between the old and the new, a dialogue between traditional and contemporary forms and meanings. In this way, tradition lives on and the contemporary enlarges its perspective.

Christian worship, because Christ was inclusive, should be free to include all kinds of worship resources. Today we are in a worship rut. We often erroneously equate worship with the forms of worship. Consequently when change of form is attempted, the worshiper panics because he fears that his worship is being taken from him. Using a brokerage analogy, many worshipers are investing in only one stock (one form). That is dangerous. They need to diversify (be open to the use of all kinds of forms and other resources). Why should worship which calls for cooperation between Holy Spirit and man become so rigid and sterile? Forms are meant to be incarnations of the Spirit, not incarcerations of it. Leaders of worship may help their people keep the forms in tension with the Spirit, and therefore, responsive to re-formation, trans-formation, or even new formation.

The forms of worship are the minimum rather than the maximum provision. What is written, as in a prayer book, is only the skeleton of worship, not worship itself. The skeleton must be clothed with feelings, meanings, acts, and thoughts that represent the person in dialogue with his fellows and God. Slavish conformity to the letter of the form stifles spiritual growth of both leader and congregation. Spaces can be provided between parts of the service in which silence, guided meditation, and nonverbal expression can be used to bring people's meanings into dialogue with the meanings that are potentially present in the form. Before saying a general confession, for example, time could be provided for people to focus on some specific aspect of their "dark side" for which they are sorry, and then with that focus repeat the verbal form of confession. Or, when they have heard the words of assurance that they are forgiven, take a moment to ask, "Since we have received forgiveness, will we resolve to give forgiveness to others during the coming week?"

The creative tension between the traditional and the contemporary is essential for creating worship that is equally expressive of the meanings of God and those of man. Some contemporary innovative worship has been unbalanced, too sensory, too human-centered, and too neglectful of the full religious dimension. We need worship that helps us come into the presence of the Lord and all his meanings with the fullness of the meaning of what it is now to be human. Worship must be a high point of awareness, of presence, of meaning. Presence means a sense of self, of others, and of the environment in and between which the Spirit of God moves and makes us aware of the fullest potential of relationship. Meaning is the awareness of that presence and its relation to our thoughts, feelings, expectations, responsibilities, and our power to endure and to achieve. Men need such awareness to survive the harsh moments of present and future testing.

Men live in two worlds: the outward and the inward. Worship must be sacramental. The outward thing or act signifies an inner meaning. This principle is built into creation, but the ridiculous controversies and prejudices about sacraments have robbed us of the universal basis of the nature of creation. Without the sacramental principle, making sense of sacraments is impossible. The stone is more than stone. It is energy; it has history; in a sense it is God because God is in it, just as the craftsman is in what he makes. Bread is more than bread, it is life and has the power to nourish. It represents both the creation of God and the creativity of man. Therefore, bread is God and man. Also, I am my body and my body is I. This sacramental character of all nature has implications for issues of ecology, and our relation to and use of our physical environment. When men piously eat bread and drink wine in memory and honor of their Lord, and exploit and destroy the soil, air, and light which is the source of that bread, they are hypocritical.

Thus worship must restore the unity of body and soul; of man and nature; of past, present, and future; of form and vitality; of outward sign and inner meaning in order

that the inevitable and constant dialogue between God
and man may be expressed more fully and celebratingly.

There can be a kind of worship where God and man
really meet in moments when the whole human enterprise seems to make sense. These moments cannot be
created: they are the gift of the Spirit. Ministers cannot
make them. If, however, ministers and laity together
pool their personal and social powers, employ their potential freedoms of expression, and utilize both the traditional and contemporary resources available to them,
they can produce designs for worship that will be open
to the action of Spirit in the continuing work of rec-
onciling and reuniting of life. Religion, and therefore
worship, needs to be inclusive of all that man is, of all
that God gives, of all the ways that men express their
repentance, love, and hope. We need to be reverently
and courageously experimental.

Inclusionists are concerned about structures, but adaptable ones. They are free to let die what needs to die, and
open to what needs to be born. Out of the meaning of
what has happened in the past, in relation to the meaning of what is happening now, and in anticipation of the
meaning of that which is to come, they create their
response in worship.

"Growing" Your God

One reason why many church people drag their feet
in relation to the changes in the world is that they have
too narrow and rigid a concept of God. Men unfortunately tend to equate God's Person with their limited
concepts of God. They do the same thing in relation to
the Divine Being that they do in relation to each other,
namely, confuse their subjective perceptions with the
fullness of the reality that they perceive. Exclusionists

thus tend to turn their God into an exclusionist, fashioning him according to their prejudices and limitations. (J. B. Phillips examined this phenomenon in detail in his book *Your God Is Too Small.*) It is interesting to observe that an exclusionist's understanding of God grows smaller and smaller the longer he lives.

Whatever we mean by God, it must mean that he is a power of being greater than our capacity to think and feel, love, understand, interpret, or express; and we need to be very careful to distinguish between God as he is in himself and our fragile thoughts about what he is like. We should honor him as we are bidden to honor one another.

He who would be truly religious and hold inclusionist attitudes toward who God is, will remain open to the promptings of his spirit as experienced in the varied relationships of living. Attitudes of humility are required not only with respect to our own convictions but with respect to the convictions of others. Inclusionists should also be open to learning from others' experiences of religious truth and the implications of such experience for them and all men. They should have attitudes of reverence for the mystery and wonder of all that the name of God at its best seems to suggest.

As in the case of relationships with other human beings, inclusionists expect to find their relationship to God change, develop, and grow. One might even say, "Their God grows" because they work at "growing" their God. I realize that this sounds like an egocentric kind of relationship with God, and yet as in the case of human relationships, this truly describes the process. God is what he is to us, in spite of the fact that within himself he is infinitely more. It is imperative, therefore, that we have this attitude of "growing" in relationship to him. Growing in our understanding as response to our ex-

perience of his love, mercy, and forgiveness; of his act of
faith in man in turning over to him the gifts of his creation; and of his passion to help and save man. Our growing concept of God should make us more patient, tolerant, caring, courageous, forgiving, and genuinely and
fully human. Our growing concept of God should diminish bigotry, intolerance, defensiveness, the need to
be right. As we grow in our relationship to God, we
should find it easier to decide in favor of our own growth,
and we should find ourselves stronger in resisting the
temptation to hide behind and shelter our little gods
from the God who is.

It is the very nature of God to reveal himself. We can
receive this revelation only within ourselves, and in response to our experiences in our relations with nature and
man. I must, therefore, accept that "my" God will be
different from "your" God. At first, this sounds divisive
and isolated. Actually there is a very rich sense of relationship among people who are really in a growing relationship with God, because the more they grow, the
more they grow toward one another. Exclusionists move
toward disunity and diversification; and inclusionists
move toward unification and community.

Thus, when I say a creed, for example, I can only
profess what I understand it to mean, and every other
person in the congregation does the same. I must strive,
and so must others, to grow my relationship to God in
such a way that every time I say the creed, I understand
its symbolism more fully and more responsibly. Being a
member of a living church should be a source of comfort
because I am a part of a fellowship of growing people
who together respond to life and affirm its truths. Together we contemplate the mysteries more fully than
each can ever do by himself. Others believe and practice
for me what I cannot, and I believe and practice for

them what they cannot. We have in this relationship a fellowship of inclusionists growing their understanding of and trust in God, responsive to his Spirit, open to change, freed from the domination of inherited form, and willing to surrender the obsolete in favor of that which is in the process of becoming. These are Spirit-led people, and together they constitute a core of life-practitioners who possess resources that will enable them to cope more adequately with accelerating change and its perplexing problems. Upon such a core of believers, the future of the human race may well depend. Men today are asking for a faith that will be open to every human being, and help bring into some kind of correlation our knowledge, technology, and relational capacity. Whether this core of believers will continue to bear our present denominational identities remains to be seen. Possibly the church as we now know it will eventually disappear, so that if we were to return to the earth in a hundred years, we might not recognize the institutional forms in which the faith we now know will reside. But I am *sure* that we would recognize the enduring truth of our faith, even though its form and communication changed. If an exclusionist were to return in a hundred years, he would be dismayed because the changes would obscure for him the truth.

Our religion and worship need also to become more ecumenical. "Ecumenical" means "world inclusive"— inclusive of the truth in all religions. After two thousand years of divisions and fragmentation among ourselves, we are now beginning to unify and center the understandings and expressions of our Judeo-Christian faith and traditions. This is good but not enough. Many people who have been alienated from Western Christianity and Judaism are turning to Eastern religion for inspiration and guidance, and thus are indicating a new possibility in the dimension of ecumenism and a new example of religious inclusion. People in our own tradition who have ceased to pray or engage in any kind of devotional life are turning to meditation, yoga, and other resources. The question is: Can we, out of the security that our faith is supposed to give us, risk communication with other faiths and disciplines? If the Christian believes, for example, that Christ is the Lord of life, why can he not be undefensive and open his mind and heart to other ways of life in the firm conviction that there can be no contradictions between truths? Truth can only be incomplete, never contradictory. If it seems to be in conflict, it is only because we have not as yet found the point of correlation. Holding our various faiths and their truths in complementary relation will increase the power of men to survive change, conflict, and ambiguity, and to shape a new social environment for human growth and actualization.

We need religious vision and power now when all institutions seem corrupt, when all men seem out for themselves, when death seems the welcome end, when changes make us hopeless strangers in a world where the pressures of time and responsibility seem to displace the possibilities of grace and love.

10. Living Inclusively for Survival

If we are to survive our contemporary conflicts, confusions, and ambiguities and become a society favorable to actualization of human potential, we will have to change our way of living, our values, and our goals. Human survival depends upon regulation and stabilization of birth rate, finding ways of protecting and developing our natural resources, eliminating war as a solution to anything, eliminating the possibilities of atomic suicide, redirecting the purposes of education from economic-military interests to humanitarian and relational concerns, and finally, if possible, upon exhuming from beneath hierarchical and doctrinal rubbish the essence of religion as life-affirming and other than life-denying.

Our theme is that the aforementioned tasks call for inclusionist rather than exclusionist living. With inclusionists rests the hope for survival, and beyond that, the flourishing of man and his society. Each of us has to ask ourselves at this point: "Which am I—exclusionist or inclusionist? Which am I predominantly? And which of these am I more and more becoming? Am I building shelters into which I can escape from life, or do I have some capacity to face the risks of growth, the death of some forms, habits, attitudes, convictions, and allegiances for the sake of new life?" Dare we to ask questions that will move us and others into more life rather than away from it, that will open us to new truth that corrects and completes what we have thought was true?

How Does One Live Inclusively?

But is not this inclusionist theme too individually focused to be effective in relation to the vast and complex problems that confront men now? On first thought it might seem so. Not so, though, when we remember that the power of the individual is needed to create, maintain, and run the machine and the organization. Nor does the inclusionist power depend upon the existence of charismatic leaders. Actually, the charismatic leader often excludes the inclusionist power of the people by developing hero-worship that is accompanied by and ends in resentment and rejection, because it creates dependency which immobilizes the creative power of group leadership. Our situation now calls for the participation of men and women at all levels of life—politicians, government leaders, educators, industrialists, professionals of all kinds, labor leaders, voters and activists—who have the courage to embody in their thinking, feeling, and work the principle of inclusion as a way of addressing the problems of this earth at the level where they encounter them. Thus will organizations, institutions, decisions, programs, and purposes change because people are changing, and changing other people. We are faced with the task of a new evangelism: not the old petty evangelism of the Bible thumper or denominational promoter but the evangelism that sees the vision of a new heaven and a new earth in which the crucified will be uncrucified and men will be free to move experimentally to a new level of human endeavor and achievement.

This will call for an inclusionist attitude toward the different stages through which men pass from birth to death. In the younger years, children are more naturally inclusionist. There is, first, the dependent period where we learn our lessons from watching others, imitating and testing the way in which they respond to life. It is then that we receive the early lessons in both exclusionism or inclusionism from the examples provided us by our parents and others. Then follows the period of youth: a time of exploration of our own and others' powers and of the nature of the world in which we live; a time to try ourselves out in relation to the resources that are available to us both within and outside ourselves; a time for the achievement of identity, of a sense of relationship, and its possibilities. Then come the middle years, which are a time of consolidation, participation, and action. Under stress we may begin to lose our courage, to compromise; to become reactionary and make exclusionist decisions. These are the dangerous years when we may settle for what we know and turn our faces away from all that we *might* learn and know. Instead, they may be years of increasing interest, vigor, and a sense of possibility. Old age follows, which can be a time of continued action, increased wisdom, reflection, and appreciation of being, if inclusion is practiced during the earlier stages of the individual's life. Exclusionism, however, produces a bitter, bigoted, bile-producing old age.

Each age—childhood, youth, middle age, and old age

—needs and can teach each other. Young people live not only with youth, but with middle-aged and elderly people, which can cause repeated occasions of misunderstanding and separation. Such tragedies of separation can be prevented by the principle of inclusion, as we learn to be complements to one another. "The impatience of youth needs the restraining influence of experience, which knows that change is not always for the better, but the smugness of experience needs to force itself to be honest with the young and to admit that what they want for this world is pretty much what we want, too, whenever we are not too tired or too indifferent to care." (Editorial, *Detroit Free Press*, December 26, 1969.)

We come now to the question: How do I become an inclusionist, especially when I may have been an exclusionist for years? There is also the prior question: How do I know when I am being exclusionist?

I know that I am exclusionist: (*a*) when I cannot accept criticism from others as a possible guide for growth; (*b*) when I habitually succumb to the fear of anything new and am prevented from examining its possibilities for me and others; (*c*) when I live my life safely and avoid risking it for growth and the accomplishment of new goals; (*d*) when I look for things to return to normal and for the good old days. Every person and organization needs to have dependable means of feedback: sources that help us to see ourselves as we are, to evaluate our way of living for its health and effectiveness. The difficulty is that exclusionists, not wanting to change and grow, will be oblivious to the need for checking on their way of living. In some situations and at some time, however, such a person will be confronted by his head-in-the-sand way of life. Then it is to be hoped that he will heed the signs and make some changes.

Changing from exclusionist to inclusionist means

changing from a life based on fear to a life based on trust;
from being a closed person to being an open person; from
being motivated by a sense of oughtness to being a self-
determining, deciding person; from being a controlling
individual to becoming an interactive one who is willing
to participate with others in relationships of trust.

The question I am asking: "How does one become
an inclusionist?" is best answered positively and with
illustrations. A good place to begin is with oneself. Ask
yourself: Am I the kind of person who values being right
over and above being in relation? If so, why don't I try
to focus my interest on the person who disagrees with
me? What in his life explains his point of view? How
do I feel about this person apart from the issue under
debate? What, if anything, would I like to give this
person besides my opinion? What in his opinion does
my opinion need? What in his personality complements
who I am? Maybe I really would rather "switch" (be
open to change) than "fight" (to control). Is the fighting worth all that I am losing in possible relationship to
that person?

Or, take the matter of one's need to control people
and situations. What fears keep me from letting go the
controls? Why not try letting others make decisions?
Why not try doing things their way for a change? Try
letting myself be cared for, instead of feeling that I
always have to care for others. Do I really have to pretend being what I am not in order to keep (in my esti-
mation) on top of the situation? Why not experiment
with the joy of having my competencies and achievements complemented by those of others? Try surrendering my isolation and loneliness for companionship and
community. In other words, why don't I try to move
from attitudes and positions of fear to those of trust?

Another way of becoming an inclusionist is by being

aware of your feelings and including them in your relationships, instead of denying them and pretending that they do not exist. You have both positive and negative feelings. As we have seen, they are the two sides of our feelings, and negative feelings need to be included and, as often as possible, subordinated to the positive. If you are angry because you are hurt, these feelings can be used positively by recognizing them and admitting them to yourself and others as something you have to deal with. If you have feelings of love and affection, try to acknowledge them by expressing them appropriately. Much of the loneliness and misery of life is a result of failure to recognize and deal with feelings which need to be included as a part of the agenda of all relationships. Recently someone with sensitive perception asked me how I was feeling. My first response was to say, "Oh, all right." Then I realized that I was covering up feelings that were disturbing me and by so doing, shutting myself off from possible help. Fortunately, I was able to add, "No, that is not true. I'm really troubled and in need of help." When at that friend's invitation I shared my disturbed feelings, I did receive help. This was an experience of mutual inclusion that has tremendous power for healing.

We can deal with our emotions by staying with them until they have been expressed and their meaning explored. (By "expression" I do not mean venting, which is selfish and destructive.) In a marriage, for instance, feelings can be a barrier, but if dealt with they can be a resource for quickening and deepening the relationship. The results depend on the freedom of the partners to accept feelings and to use them as a part of the curriculum of their relationship. By curriculum I mean use them as a source for learning and growth. The more versatile the feelings and the more complete their expression, the richer the relationship will be. In this day when so much emphasis is put upon expression of negative feelings, I want to stress as well the importance of expressing positive feelings. Sometimes, of course, negative feelings have to be expressed and dealt with before we are free to express our positive ones.

You can become an inclusionist by keeping your convictions growing. A conviction is a belief to which we have been persuaded by a process of education reinforced by experience. We all have convictions which are our guides and stabilizers, our fixed points in the fluid and changing meanings and values that surround us. Our convictions about ourselves, for example, determine what we think about ourselves and our possibilities. They determine how we behave, the kind of possibilities we attempt, and the kinds of efforts we will try to make.

Living convictions are convictions that are still growing and changing. Young people often rebel against the values and attitudes and convictions of their parents. If these parental convictions are growing ones, the chances are that the young people later on will embody them as their own—of course, with their own changes and adaptations. If parental convictions do not seem authentic, they may be permanently repudiated, or later accepted because the young people do not have anything else to fall back on. It is important to have one's own convictions about oneself, about others, about God, the purpose of life, and one's role in it.

Convictions are an area in which the principles of exclusion and inclusion are most pertinent. Some people hold their convictions rigidly and exclusively. They are closed to all new data and meaning that might alter their convictions. Because they are afraid to change, they hold their convictions defensively, but represent themselves as being right-minded and strong. Actually they become more and more dogmatic because their convictions are embedded in a tradition that is not in dialogue with contemporary need and demand. The person with exclusively held convictions is not going anywhere. He has arrived. Not even the spirit of God can move him. His epitaph will be, "Here lies one whose convictions became prejudices."

In contrast, convictions can be held inclusively, that is, held openly and responsively in relation to new values, needs, conditions, and responsibilities. It is good for us to be able to say, "My beliefs have grown; I can embrace more truth from different sources than I was able to do earlier in my life. I am more tolerant of the convictions of others and can see how theirs have helped to strengthen mine. I am happy that differences of conviction can be complementary rather than divisive. I look forward to further growth because I know how possible it is to outgrow convictions once held."

It will help you to acquire inclusionist capacities if you will strive to develop more versatility in your tastes, interests, ideas, reading, skills, and relationships. Some older people keep growing by working at something new each year and are able to retrain and even increase a flexibility and openness of spirit that helps to compensate for whatever physical deterioration is experienced. The decision to be an inclusionist early in life is a big factor in determining the kind of old age a person will have: creative or despondent; hopeful or bitter; loved and loving or lonely. Retirement, which for many seems to occur earlier and earlier, presents problems especially for men who have depended on their jobs to give structure if not some meaning to their lives.

Finally, one can become an inclusionist by trying to find more options or possibilities for decision and action. We all have a tendency to think in terms of either-or alternatives, which is an exclusionist way of thinking. "Should I," writes a woman, "reconcile myself to a bad marriage or get a divorce?" Before either of these alternatives is chosen, she can look at her situation again and see what other choices she has. For example, she can consult a marriage counselor; she can ask, "What am I doing that makes my situation seem so impossible?" and try to improve her own performance; she can find other relationships, interests, and resources that may give her fulfillments that for the moment do not seem possible with her husband; by decreasing her dependency on her husband and therefore her resentment of him, she may produce a change in him. These and other possible options will deliver her from the dilemma of a sterile either-or choice. The same search for added options in any matter—political, social, psychological, educational, or behavioral—is inclusionist and will make survival and growth possible.

Fruits of Inclusion

One of the first fruits of inclusion is the achievement of a capacity for a *mature kind of security*. Earlier it was pointed out that exclusionists have a primitive kind of security based on what was called "deficiency" needs, such as the need to be right. The opposite, or inclusionist, is aware that he has within himself the capacity to deal with strange and challenging situations. A friend has told me that he is sufficiently secure to know that no matter what happens to him and those with whom he is associated, he will be able to respond to it in some constructive way. He is secure enough to include himself in any situation and any situation in himself. He has developed creative powers of survival. The mature security of a family enables it to face all kinds of experiences within and without, including the possibility that its form may have to change in order that its life may be preserved. Changed circumstances such as moving to a new area and house, death of a parent, departure of children, loss or increase of income require changed patterns of living. The mature security of a church would leave it free to change its forms of worship or action or faith in the interests of the changing needs that confront it. The mature security of a teacher would open him to the possibility of responding to his pupil as a human being even if it meant for the moment abandoning the agenda that the curriculum required. The mature security of a corporation would be expressed in its ability to accept criticism and to revise its organization and purposes in consultation with its critics. The mature security of a labor union could be expressed in a willingness to forgo the usual gains that it expects in negotiations for the sake of the national good.

Obviously this kind of security is not too common. At least the news of it does not frequently appear in the newspapers. The future of our society, however, depends upon the prevalence of that kind of mature security. We have to face the fact that only a small proportion of the population possesses growth security, and that they will have to use it in behalf of the majority of the population that lacks it. Actually, the latter have no awareness of the possibility of such maturity. The truly privileged in our society are those who are capable of the kinds of insights we are talking about, and it is the responsibility of such a privileged group to practice what they are capable of for the sake of themselves and others.

A second fruit of inclusionism is the *satisfaction of achievement*. In the midst of the risks which the practice of inclusionism requires, there appear now and then solid and real achievements which are a source of enormous satisfaction. A marriage that has survived years of testing and vicissitude emerges with an increased sense of trust and possibility. Out of the struggle for survival and growth, made up as it is of experiences of both achievement and failure, is forged a sense of identity, authenticity, perspective, and wisdom. A sense of wonder, reverence, and humility emerges out of the same struggle, in the midst of which our achievements are the product of the interaction of thought, feeling, and action.

Achievement is never the accomplishment of a single individual, but always takes place in the context of relationship. The more inclusive those relationships are, the greater the achievement. I might be tempted to think that the writing of this book is the achievement of myself alone, but that thought is erroneous, because it has to be written out of interaction and with the help of many others. The artist in his studio or the president of a corporation in the seemingly isolated splendor of his office accomplishes not out of his singleness, but out of his capacity to be in touch with, and responsive to, all kinds of individuals, organizations, and environments.

Achievement is often thought of in terms of "works" of one kind or another, but the greatest achievement of all, which lies behind all the works, is the achievement of becoming a fully human being: to be able to say, "I am who I am," with increasing awareness of meaning and an increasing capacity to be, and to be in relation.

This leads us to the third fruit of inclusion, which is *participation in community*. What do we mean by community? Community is orchestrated individuality. In other words, the achievement of being is an underlying necessity for the achievement of community. The achievement of individuality is indispensable, and is the fruit of inclusion: that is, the fruit of being able to affirm oneself while at the same time accepting responsible criticism of oneself; of being able to grow one's sense of self-worth and take it into every enterprise of which one is a part. This means having a sense of integrity, being able to regulate one's behavior from within—not having to be ruled from without—and therefore being relieved of the need to rebel against unwanted authority. The sense of tyranny, whether real or not, destroys the sense of self as a creative source of life. Rebellion is the act of a threatened person. Revolution, in contrast, is the act of an authentic person, acting responsibly and con- structively against the exclusionist forces in society that are the enemies of actualization in life. Therefore revolu- tion may be necessary and healthful for the growth of community.

Community—or orchestrated individuality—is always in the process of being renewed and rediscovered. The human soul is restless when it has to live without com- munity, because it cannot be satisfied with singleness while its very nature cries out for being in relation, being a part of a larger growth process. Upon this emergence of community—or to use a religious term, kingdom of God —depends the future of mankind, in both its individual and its corporate manifestations. Thus the hope of life calls for volunteers to live inclusively.

And so finally, a fruit of inclusion is an ever expand- ing *awareness of the Infinite* in our midst. Awareness in- cludes not only an awareness of ourselves and other human beings in their various organizations and enter- prises, but also an awareness of a presence that cannot be explained by what we can see, analyze, measure, and understand. Man gives different names to this mystical, elusive, and yet powerful presence, without which he feels lonely, and in response to which he gains a new grasp on the possibilities of being, becoming, achieving, and living. New dimensions that transcend human dimensions seem to open before him. This inclusionist possibility is beautifully described by Gibran:

Who can separate his faith from his actions, or his belief from his occupations?

Who can spread his hours before him, saying, "This for God and this for myself; This for my soul, and this other for my body?"

All your hours are wings that beat through space from self to self.

He who wears his morality but as his best garment were better naked. . . .

And he who defines his conduct by ethics imprisons his song-bird in a cage.

The freest song comes not through bars and wires.

And he to whom worshipping is a window, to open but also to shut, has not yet visited the house of his soul whose windows are open from dawn to dawn.*

Survival? Yes, it is possible; but only through growth, the willingness to risk what is, for the sake of what is yet to happen.

---

* Kahlil Gibran, *The Prophet* (New York: Alfred A. Knopf, 1923), pp. 87–88.